The House that Jack Built

100 Years of the House of Townend

John Townend

Highgate of Beverley
Highgate Publications (Beverley) Limited

2006

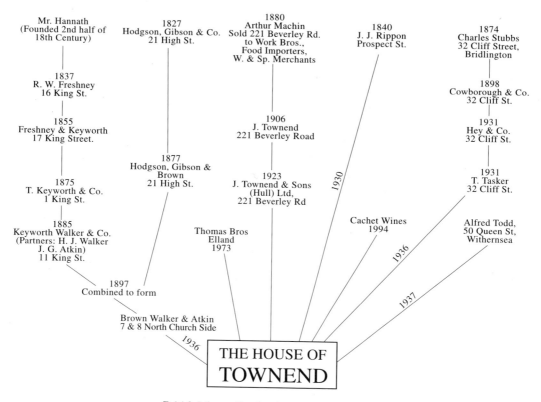

Mr. Hannath
(Founded 2nd half of
18th Century)

1827
Hodgson, Gibson & Co.
21 High St.

1880
Arthur Machin
Sold 221 Beverley Rd.
to Work Bros.,
Food Importers,
W. & Sp. Merchants

1840
J. J. Rippon
Prospect St.

1874
Charles Stubbs
32 Cliff Street,
Bridlington

1837
R. W. Freshney
16 King St.

1898
Cowborough & Co.
32 Cliff St.

1855
Freshney & Keyworth
17 King Street.

1906
J. Townend
221 Beverley Road

1931
Hey & Co.
32 Cliff St.

1877
Hodgson, Gibson &
Brown
21 High St.

1875
T. Keyworth & Co.
1 King St.

1923
J. Townend & Sons
(Hull) Ltd,
221 Beverley Rd

1931
T. Tasker
32 Cliff St.

1885
Keyworth Walker & Co.
(Partners: H. J. Walker
J. G. Atkin)
11 King St.

Thomas Bros
Elland
1973

Cachet Wines
1994

Alfred Todd,
50 Queen St,
Withernsea

1930

1936

1937

1897
Combined to form

Brown Walker & Atkin
7 & 8 North Church Side

1936

THE HOUSE OF
TOWNEND

British Library Cataloguing in Publication Data.
A catalogue record for this book is available from the British Library.

© 2006 John Townend

John Townend asserts the moral right to be identified as the author of this work.

ISBN 1 902645 6 4

Published by

Highgate of Beverley
Highgate Publications (Beverley) Limited
4 Newbegin, Beverley, HU17 8EG. Telephone (01482) 886017

Printed by Highgate Print Limited
4 Newbegin, Beverley, HU17 8EG. Telephone (01482) 886017

Preface

When I wrote this book, it was not intended to be published. It was the story of the House of Townend, written warts and all, purely for the benefit of future generations of my family and it would reside in the Company safe.

The project started some ten years ago and as it was coming to fruition, the year before we celebrated our Centenary, I was persuaded by my family to have it published as part of our Centenary celebrations.

I have written about our failures, as well as our successes. Most histories of private firms are highly sanitised and the real life battles, struggles, feuds and fallouts, which happen in all family businesses, are smoothed over; I haven't done this because it would, in my view, take the heart out of the book. Most of the people, who might be offended, are dead.

I accept that this is my view of events; others might have seen things from a different perspective, but, as the historian will tell you, 'most history is written by the winners.'

I have had an interesting and exciting life in politics and the wine trade. In retrospect, I think my first love is the wine trade; at least in business, the knives usually come from the front, not like politics, when it is invariably a stab in the back.

In business, success comes from hard work, a reputation for honesty, integrity and keeping one's word. It is rough and tough, but lots of fun.

I hope the readers of this book will enjoy it and be tolerant of the outspoken views, for which I am now well-known.

John E. Townend

Contents

First 'No. 10 Club Dinner'.

Chapter 1:

Beginning

This is the story of a firm of wine merchants and the family that owns it. For nearly 100 years the family has dominated the firm and the firm has dominated the family.

The founder, Jack Townend, was born in Hull in 1872, the third son of the large family of John Townend, (in the Townend family it was always said the first son was traditionally called John). How the third son became John we do not know. The family has no records of his education or his father's occupation, but his grandson recollects that he told him that the family originally came from the West Riding of Yorkshire. When he left school he joined Earle's shipyard in Hull, where he served his apprenticeship and eventually became a skilled man.

In those days when a ship was completed the workers were paid off until the next contract came along, when they would be recruited again. Ambitious single men, like Jack Townend, did not hang around without work. They travelled to other shipbuilding towns where work was available. This was long before Norman Tebbitt's advice to get on your bike if you wanted a job. Jack travelled up to Hartlepool and found employment in the local shipyard.

He was already making his name as an up-and-coming rugby player, playing for the Hull Rugby Club. We know from a bound copy of a history of the Hull Rugby Club printed just before the turn of the century that he scored a try playing for Hull A in 1891/2 when Hull was still an amateur rugby union club. When he arrived in Hartlepool he joined the local club and quickly became a star. When the contract at the shipyard came to an end and Jack was paid off, he told the club secretary that in a week's time he would be returning to Hull. 'You can't leave now in the middle of the season,' the secretary said. 'You are our best player.' 'Well I can't live on thin air, the ship is finished and I am going back to Hull to get work,' said Jack. 'Don't worry,' said the Secretary. 'We will see you are all right.' On Saturday in Jack's boots were some sovereigns, certainly more than his weekly wage. This was boot money that led eventually to the formation of the Northern League and the advent of professional Rugby League. His finances assured, Jack stayed and played for Hartlepool until the end of the season.

When Jack returned to Hull he rejoined Hull Rugby Football Club and stayed with them when the club went professional in 1894/5. The family has in its possession a photograph of the Hull First Team that played against Leeds in 1895/6, which included not only Jack but also

Alderman Jack Townend, founder and first Chairman

his brother Charlie. Jack was Vice Captain in 1898 and another photograph of the whole team that played Hull Kingston Rovers in 1901/2 names him as the Captain.

He and his brother, Charlie Townend, had the distinction of playing for Hull RFC and Hull Kingston Rovers RFC on the same day. It was on a Bank Holiday and they played for their own Club, Hull, in the morning and for Hull KR as guest players in the afternoon because they were short of players. Jack made 144 appearances for Hull and scored 58 tries.

He always played stand-off half and his younger brother Charlie played scrum-half. When in 1899 his wife produced twin boys, the headline on the sports page of the *Hull Daily Mail* was 'Two new half-backs for Hull'. They were christened John and Charles after their father and uncle. Despite the tradition, the eldest twin was

Team photograph of Hull v Hull Kingston Rovers 1900-01 – where Jack Townend, captain, is holding the ball.

Jack Townend on the bike for five cyclists. (Second from the front).

christened Charles, because he seemed to be rather sickly and wasn't expected to live and the youngest twin was christened Jack. Ironically, Charles lived far longer than his twin brother and turned out to be much the stronger.

Jack was a top cycle racer and won the One Mile and Five Mile Championships of the East Riding of Yorkshire and North Lincolnshire and prizes to the value of £250. He was also a gambler and he used to bet on himself. He told the story of how he used to save himself until the odds he could get on himself were very good and only then would he bet on himself and really go out to win. Throughout his life he liked to gamble and one occasion, when he went to Beverley Races, he had had a bad day and by the end of the last race but one had lost all his cash. He sold his return ticket, put the proceeds on the last race and lost. As a result, he had to walk home all the way from Beverley to Hull.

He decided he would cash in on his popularity as a sportsman and go into business and in 1893 became the tenant of a public house in Dock Street called Good Ship Molly. At the age of 21 he was the youngest licensee in Hull. He changed the name of the public house to the Rugby Hotel around 1899.

In order to build up business, as soon as he came off the pitch after an away game he would telegraph the result to the pub. Customers would come in from far and wide to get the result well before the evening paper was on the streets and, of course, while they were waiting they were drinking his beer. Whilst he was single his pub was looked after by his sisters when he was away playing rugby and cycling. He started a trend, which went all the way through his business life; he always gave jobs to the family but he wasn't noted for overpaying them. Because he was such a successful sportsman he was the family hero and his brothers and sisters would do anything for him.

On 25 September 1898 he married Alice Hope, the fifth daughter of Robert Hope of Hull, at St. Katherine's Church, Milford Haven. Prior to her marriage she had worked at Barnby and Rust, jeweller's in the Market Place. Alice was a very confident, vivacious young lady who during her lifetime had a great love of clothes and jewellery. One day Mr. Rust, the proprietor of the shop,

left her in charge with another young assistant. They were very quiet, there were no customers, and, egged on by the young girl, Alice started dressing herself up in the most expensive jewellery, rings, bracelets, necklace and finally a tiara. She had just placed it on her head when the boss came back. He looked at her over his spectacles, picked up the papers he had left and as he was going out said, 'Miss Hope, fine feathers make fine birds!'

We know Jack was at the Rugby Hotel until 1900 when he moved to the Bull Hotel on Beverley Road near the Beverley Road Baths. This was a Moor's and Robson's house. In the early years of the century he decided to expand his business by starting to bottle Guinness and he opened a new business in small premises down Temple Street under the name J. Townend, Stout Bottler. Despite being tied to the brewery he started putting his own Guinness into the Bull. After about a year, in 1906, the brewery suddenly woke up to the fact that he hadn't bought any Guinness for over a year. Upon investigation they found out what had happened and terminated his tenancy forthwith. He was in quite a predicament; he had a young family and nowhere to live. He solved the problem by buying a nearby licensed grocer's, Work Bros., at 221 Beverley Road on the corner of Cave Street.

This business had been founded on this site in 1876 by Mr. James Work. In the Directory *Modern Hull*, published in 1893, they are described as importers of teas and coffee, family grocers and provision dealers, wine, spirit, ale and stout merchants. The Directory then goes on to say, 'The whole of Messrs. Work Bros. establishments are handsomely fitted up, displaying to great advantage immense stocks of high class goods consisting of hams, cheese, butter, eggs, lard, large quantities of various kinds of foreign produce, dried fruits, spices, tinned and potted goods, green fruit of all kinds, bread, biscuits, confectionery of every description, wines, spirits and malt liqueurs from the leading breweries and distilleries. The firm are also agents for Messrs. W. & A. Gilbey and keep a full stock of their leading specialities. As a high class business Messrs. Work Bros. has no equal in the district. The arrangements are in every respect perfect, ample space and every facility is afforded for the inspection and selection of goods. Customers have their orders promptly and carefully carried out. The business is an extensive one patronised by the leading gentry, clergy, commercial and professional classes throughout the town and district.'

The family moved to 221 Beverley Road and lived in the flat over the shop. His wife ran the shop as Jack continued developing his small stout bottling business. The shop traded as J. Townend, Grocers, Wine, Spirit, Ale and Stout Merchants, and it was from the takeover of this business that the present firm of the House of Townend dates its foundation.

Jack continued to expand his beer bottling business and in 1911 a well-known local firm of beer bottlers called Faloon and Co. came onto the market when the proprietor, Mr. Robert Dawson Metcalfe, died. Jack acquired the business from this widow and moved his own business into the premises of Faloon's, which were at this time in Park Lane. It was an old established business and in the Directory, *Modern Hull,* is the following entry: 'One of the most important houses engaged in the wholesale beer trade in Hull is Messrs. Faloon and Company, whose operations extend to Yorkshire, Lincolnshire and the neighbouring counties.'

Jack now had two businesses, both sole traders; the beer bottling business trading as Faloon and Company whilst the shop continued to trade as J. Townend. Over the next decade Jack worked hard and his business prospered. In those days there were a lot of free public houses to which he sold his Guinness and stout, but Guinness would not allow the brewers who brewed stout to bottle Guinness under the Harp label. Consequently Guinness bottlers could supply nearly all the pubs whether tied or not, as the public invariably demanded the Harp label as it gave the Guinness authenticity.

His success of building up sales was undoubtedly helped by his sporting reputation, and, as so often happens, success breeds antagonism. In Jack's case, he was particularly disliked by the brewers. As already mentioned, he had been thrown out by one of the local breweries, Moor's and Robson's, and the other one, Hull Brewery, didn't like the way he undercut their prices. As a result they used to badmouth him in the trade. Jack

told the story of how he called on a prospective customer saying he was from Faloon's and tried to open an account. The proprietor said, 'Faloon's? Isn't that the business owned by Jack Townend?' 'Yes', said Jack. 'I wouldn't buy from him. He's a terrible man" 'Really,' said Jack, 'Do you know Jack Townend personally?' 'Yes,' said the landlord. I know him well'. Jack said, 'Oh, have we met?' 'No,' said the customer. 'Well,' said Jack, 'I'm Jack Townend himself.' The man was naturally embarrassed but Jack bought him a drink; they became firm friends and he became one of Faloon's best and most loyal customers in the following years.

When employing people, Jack always gave priority to members of his large family. Most of his brothers and sisters worked for him at some time or another. The best remembered was his brother Sid, known as Uncle Sid, who worked on the Guinness bottling line. Whilst the business was expanding the family was also growing. In all they had nine children. Another set of twins died in childbirth and two children died before reaching their teens. Five survived, Jack and Charles, the twins, Nan, Alice and the youngest, Alec. The children all went to Beverley Road School and from there the twins went on to Hull Grammar School. Alec was much younger and by the time he went to school Jack had prospered and could afford to send him to Hymers College.

As it was a family business the children were expected to work after school and, Charles told how he had a regular routine, arriving home from school and immediately going out and delivering shop orders to private houses on a delivery bike. It was not all work, there was some time for play and Charles used to recall how he and his brother would go into the bottling stores, which attracted rats, with air guns. They quickly discovered that if they put a bowl of Guinness on the floor and hid behind the boxes the rats came out and drank the Guinness and this made them a much easier target for the boys.

Jack Jnr. never liked school but Charles loved it. In 1913 when he was 14 years old Jack Jnr persuaded his father to let him start work, but because they were twins they always had to do the same things. If one left school they both had to leave school, so despite his pleas and protestations Charles was forced to leave the Grammar School at 14 and start work. He never wanted to go into the business, he would have liked to have stayed on at school, studied and become a doctor or an engineer, but in those days the sons of Victorian businessmen did what they were told. Father's word was law.

Although in later years Charles became successful, he never really liked the licensed trade. Jack Jnr, being considered the delicate son, ended up in the office, whereas Charles went first into the warehouse and then drove a horse and wagon delivering bottled beer and Guinness. He used to pile the wagon so high that he and his mate often had to get off and walk if they were on an uphill gradient. They used to go as far as Withernsea, which was a full day's work.

Charles Townend, the second Chairman, pilot in the Royal Flying Corps, next to his plane.

Chapter 2:

The 1914-18 war and the aftermath

By the time the Great War broke out in 1914 business had prospered to such an extent that Faloon's was the largest Guinness bottler in the area. During the war, when there were restriction, all the Guinness for the whole area was consigned to Faloon and Co. for bottling. Jack used to speak with pride of the occasion when horse-drawn lorries carrying large barrels of Guinness were lined up along Beverley Road waiting to be unloaded at the premises down Park Lane. He said they worked all night to get it bottled. Jack was too old for the Forces but in 1917 the twins joined the army. Charles had become very interested in flying and read everything he could find on the subject. He successfully applied to join the Royal Flying Corps and was trained to become a pilot. During training he and some fellow cadets were stationed at Worcester College, Oxford. In those days the planes didn't have brakes and there were no such things as parachutes. Charles said that about one-third of his intake were killed in training. He survived and got his wings and was on draft for Egypt when the Armistice was declared. He flew both Sopwith Camels and SE Scouts.

With his growing prosperity Jack had been able to purchase Kingston Villa, a large house in Pearson Park, which is now a residential home. In late 1918 or early 1919 the family moved there from the flat above the shop at Beverley Road. Subsequently Bob and Nell Buchanan were employed to run the shop. Following his family policy, Bob was Jack's nephew, the son of his wife's sister. Bob worked as a bookmaker for Habbershaw's during the day and looked after the shop in the evening while Nell looked after it from 11am to 3 pm in the day. Licensing hours at that time were restricted for retail shops to 11am to 3pm and 6pm to 10 pm. Bob became successful and his wife didn't need to work so they left the shop, which was then taken over by Bob's sister and her husband, Mona and Bob Barker. Eventually Bob left Habbershaw's and founded his own bookmaking business in Cottingham.

Before the war all the deliveries had been made by horse-drawn drays but during the war there had been considerable development of the internal combustion engine for transporting goods. Jack realised he would have to move from horse-drawn vehicles to motor lorries. With considerable foresight he decided he needed someone who understood engines and who could maintain these new-fangled vehicles. He arranged, therefore, with one of his friends, Bill Thompson, who was the pioneer of the motor trade in Hull, that Charles would go into his garage and he would teach him everything he needed to know about motor lorries. He kept his word and when after six months Charles came back he was almost a trained mechanic who could do major jobs such as changing a big end. Charles went back to driving and Jack Jnr stayed in the office.

When Charles first came back from the war he happened to meet up with Dorothy Taylor, who had been a school friend of his two sisters when her family had lived nearby in Park Road. Indeed, Dorothy in later life said Charles used to pull her pigtails when she was a schoolgirl. Now she was a vivacious dark-haired 17-year-old. Charles in his smart pilot's uniform seemed much more attractive than Charlie Townend driving his horse and rulley. They started going out together and eventually Charles asked her to marry him.

Her father, Dick Taylor, was a well-known auctioneer and estate agent practising as Richard E. Taylor FAI. Like Jack Townend he was a self-made man but his background was middle class. His father had been a master stonemason and was in business in Caistor, Lincolnshire. Unfortunately, he had died when Dick was only 18 months old and Dick was the youngest of a large family. His mother was left with the daunting prospect of bringing all these children up. Initially the business continued and the widow appointed a manager. Unfortunately the manager absconded with most of the

funds and the business collapsed. Dick's mother was left penniless with a large family to raise. There was no social security in those days and the family suffered real poverty. This experience scarred Dick for the rest of his life. When he was a relatively wealthy man he couldn't bring himself to spend money on his own comfort. The widow Taylor moved the family from Caistor to Hull, and we don't really know why. She kept them from starvation by taking in washing and sewing. All the children had to work from an early age to keep the wolf from the door.

Dick left school as early as possible by passing the school leaving examination. He worked in book keeping and collecting rents. He started his own business whilst he was still legally a minor and was only able to do so because his brother, who had emigrated to New Zealand, acted as a nominee for him.

He worked hard and became very successful. He built up a large rent roll collecting the rents of several thousand houses. That brought in a lot of work, valuation of properties and sales of properties and eventually he moved into property auctioneering.

During the Great War most of his staff, which was all male, joined the Forces. That left a void and so Dorothy, his daughter, left school and joined the practice. She was very bright and quick to learn and speedily established herself in what had previously been an all-male world. Jack Townend, who was friendly with Dick Taylor, was said to have remarked to Dick, 'That daughter of yours is a really bright go-ahead lass. I wish she belonged to me.' Little did he know that she would end up as his daughter-in-law.

Dorothy did everything the men had done and when only 16 she was going round some of the toughest slum areas in Hull collecting rents in cash. In all the seven or eight years she did this she was never once attacked or molested. How times have changed for the worse! Nowadays you wouldn't let a 16-year-old girl wander around an estate in Hull collecting rents.

In the 1920s the professional classes considered they were a cut above those in trade. Dorothy marrying into trade was considered to be marrying beneath herself. To make matters worse, at this time Charles was driving his beloved motor lorry and the height of his ambition was to maximise the number of beer cases he could get onto the vehicle. When he proposed to Dorothy she made it clear that, although she was in love with him, she wasn't going to marry a lorry driver, so he had better do something about it.

Charles decided to talk it over with his father to see if he would allow him to go into the office. Jack Jnr, who had been in the office since before the war, objected. The story goes that the two brothers ended up having a fight, which started when Charles hurled a wad of pound notes at Jack Jnr There were pound notes flying all over the place. It became clear to their father that they would find great difficulty in working together and it was decided that Jack would continue with Faloon's. The business at 221 Beverley Road, as well as having a retail licence, had a wholesale licence that was dormant, so it was decided that Charles would take over J. Townend and develop a wholesale wine and spirit business. In the early days he would be a representative for Faloon and at the same time solicit wine and spirit orders for J. Townend. When Charles told the ambitious Dorothy of these changes to his career she agreed to marry him.

Dorothy was a very active member of the Wesleyan Church and taught a Sunday school class. As with many idealistic young people, she signed the pledge never to drink alcohol, despite the fact that there was no tradition of teetotalism in her family. Indeed, Dick Taylor regularly went out for a drink leaving his wife having a glass of stout at home. When she got engaged Dorothy decided she could not remain a Wesleyan when she was marrying someone in the drink business and they would be living on the profits from the sale of alcoholic beverages. They therefore decided to get married at All Saints, which was Charles' parish church. The wedding, in 1924, was a large affair. The local M.P. was present together with numerous other local dignitaries. By this time the fathers of both the bride and groom had gone into politics and public life. Dick had been a member of the Sculcoates Board of Guardians and was now the Chairman and was also the Chairman of the Central Hull Conservative Association. Jack was also an active Conservative and would shortly be elected to Hull City Council.

Jack was now approaching 50. He had two good businesses. His family were working for him so he started to work fewer hours and looked to expand his horizons. His opportunity came when in 1924 the Councillor for Park Ward, in which Jack resided, died. There would have to be a by-election and Jack decided to stand. He had always been a committed Conservative and he used to say to his grandson, 'Don't let the Socialists mislead you into thinking all the working class were poor in the

PARK WARD BYE-ELECTION.

LADIES AND GENTLEMEN,

I have been requested by a number of Ratepayers to offer myself for the vacancy created by the regrettable death of your late esteemed representative Counc. W. W. Bulay. Having resided and carried on business in the Ward for 20 years, I claim to have a very intimate knowledge of its requirements.

Whilst refraining from making extensive "Election Promises," I fully realise that the complexity and magnitude of the tasks before the Corporation today, require that your representative should bring to bear upon each question, as it arises, a sound unselfish judgment and cast his vote on the side which promises the greatest good for the community at large rather than for any particular section. Should you honour me with your confidence by returning me as your representative on Wednesday next, I will faithfully endeavour to follow this policy.

In general terms I may describe myself as an Economist, believing that at the present time, and in the light of recent statements as to the City's financial commitments the greatest consideration must be given before sanctioning any scheme involving large expenditure.

I might add however, that I am prepared to give such consideration to any scheme which in my judgment is urgently required for the City's welfare or development.

I am,

Kingston Villa,   Ladies and Gentlemen.

Pearson Park,   Your obedient Servant,

August 20th, 1924.   **J. TOWNEND.**

Printed and Published by J. E Westoby. 8 Trinity House Lane, Hull

Election Address for J. Townend, the resident candidate, 1924.

Victorian era. I was a shipyard worker and we were the aristocrats of the working class, building ships for the world and as long as we were in work we lived very well.' He admitted if you didn't have a job life was hard, but, being a hardworking craftsman who would travel, he was never unemployed.

At that time, politics had not taken over in local government although Labour candidates were starting to appear. He stood as an Independent and described himself as the resident candidate. Below is his communication to the electors, which is of interest, particularly the style and quality of the language. He left 'board' school, as ordinary schools were called, at the age of 14, with a high level of literacy. Compare this with the average 18-year-old comprehensive school leaver, who can't spell and whose knowledge of grammar is minimal.

Dorothy, his new daughter-in-law, who had started canvassing for her father when a schoolgirl was his election agent and organised the campaign. All the family were enrolled together with friends and staff and every house was canvassed. Cars were made available to take electors to the polling stations. Dorothy was quite a clever cookie and, when one of the Townend cars brought two female electors to the poll, she was standing outside the polling station and heard one of them say to some friends, 'Oh, we are not voting for Townend. We just came in his car for a ride.' Whilst they were inside Dorothy told the driver not to wait and so they had to walk home. Rough justice.

Jack at this time was a tall distinguished-looking 52-year-old with an athletic figure. He had a large moustache and always wore a Homburg hat. Women found him attractive. His wife, who was a very jealous woman, ensured that they never got him in their sights. Having been in business for 30 years and being a well-known sportsman, it was not surprising that on 27 August 1924 he easily won the by-election on a low (23%) poll and became the councillor for Park Ward, which had an electorate of 4770.

The votes cast were:

J. Townend –	852
J. M. Barnett –	255
	597

Jack always got a good majority and his other Independent colleagues were quite envious of his wonderful election team. In a moment of generosity he offered the family to help a colleague. That almost caused a rebellion. The family would do it for Pa, as he was affectionately called, but not for a stranger. As the Labour Party grew in strength on the Council, the Independents found that, faced with strict party discipline, they were being marginalised. They therefore decided to form a group, which they called the Municipal Association Group (MAG), which included mainly Conservatives but also a few Liberals. Thereafter, Jack stood as an MAG candidate in Council elections.

He took his Council duties seriously and was eventually appointed Chairman of the Parks Committee in November 1931 and was also Deputy Chairman of the Water and Gas Committee. He introduced the idea of a Municipal Golf Course to the Council and, after great opposition, had the pleasure of eventually seeing it become a reality. He was proud to have been the first Captain of the Hull Municipal Golf Cub at Springhead Park. He was also a member of Hull Golf Club.

Never defeated at the polls, he was surprisingly elected Alderman in 1938. It was reported on the front page of the *Hull Daily Mail* of 7 April 1938 that 'The Anti Socialist members of the Hull City Council created a surprise at the Council Meeting of the Council when they outvoted the Socialists to elect John Townend as Alderman to succeed Alderman T. W. Kerry by 27 votes to 26. The Socialists were not at their full strength due to two recent deaths.' In those days, there was a tradition. 'Once an Alderman, always an Alderman', but this was broken after the Labour landslide in 1945, when Jack was removed with the rest of the non-Socialist Aldermen. He would have been delighted to know that after his death, John, his favourite grandson, followed him onto the City Council and then progressed to Parliament.

Charles started the wholesale wine business by buying a pipe of port and a hogshead of sherry, bottling and labelling them by hand, and storing them at the rear of the Beverley Road shop. He would then go out and visit customers to sell the wine. For delivery of wholesale orders in the early days they used Faloon's transport, while a boy on a box bike dealt with the retail orders. He quickly built up a growing business with public houses and clubs. There were very few licensed restaurants in those days. Life was mainly work. Charles did everything. During the day he called on customers, returning in the afternoon to do the bottling, order preparation and office work, a task which usually necessitated working until well into the evening. His one recreation was rugby football.

In view of the family's rugby tradition it is not surprising that Jack and Charles, who had been to a soccer school, started playing rugby on returning from the war. They joined the Hull and East Riding RUFC, the premier club of the area. Charles played stand-off half, whilst his brother Jack played scrum-half. Because his job involved loading beer boxes onto a lorry, unloading them and carrying them into cellars, Charles was very strong and became a fearsome tackler. It was always said that Jack, who was not as strong, had a heart like a lion when he was on a rugby pitch. They found that the 'Riding' was public school dominated and getting picked depended on how well you knew the committee. As a result, when a former committee man left the 'Riding' and re-formed the Hessle Rugby Club, Charles and Jack joined him. As so often happened with the Townend's, the family became involved. Charles became the captain, Jack Townend Snr. joined the committee and was the chairman for a time, and a cousin, Jackie Townend, who was a boxer, also played. After Charles retired, Jack Jnr joined Hull Kingston Rovers but only played as a professional for a short time.

The business started to develop and the first employee that Charles took on was called Charlie White, known to everyone as 'Whitey'. Whitey could turn his hand to everything other than office work and selling. He was well known in the local pub because he used to take his dog with him for a drink. Whitey would have a glass of Guinness or two, or three, and the dog would have a saucer of Guinness. They both rolled home together. Wages were low and in the summer he would leave the company and drive Hull Corporation buses until the late autumn when there was a lot of overtime, as they were bottling up stock for Christmas. This happened for a few years until Charles

got exasperated and refused to take him back. Eventually Jack Jnr gave him a job as a driver with Faloon's, where he stayed for quite a long period.

The wholesale business expanded and Charles was soon bottling a whole range of wines, mainly fortified, from every part of the Empire, Australia, South Africa and Cyprus. Much of his Empire wine was bought from Gale Lister of Leeds. He became very friendly with Mr. Willetts, their traveller, and subsequently with their Managing Director and owner, Louis Porter. This friendship had a significant effect on the history of the Company. Charles was always looking for new opportunities. He was the first person to bring British wine into Hull. British Ruby (port) was a bigger seller than British sherry because it was used in clubs and pubs to make a reasonably cheap port and lemon. It was probably the most popular drink with women at that time.

Jack's entry into public life took a considerable amount of his time and progressively he spent less and less time working in his businesses, leaving day-to-day management to the twins. As a result, Faloons, run by Jack Jnr, which was the larger business, being the engine room of the family fortunes, gradually ceased to progress and eventually in the 1930s and 1940s went into decline, culminating in its leaving family control. On the other hand the fledgling wine business run by Charles steadily developed and went from strength to strength.

In 1926 the general strike brought the country virtually to a standstill. Barrels of Guinness for bottling, the life blood of the business at that time, were transported to Hull by rail. The company had no stock when Charles heard some Guinness consigned to Faloon's was in the railway siding at Hessle. With the resourcefulness that typified him, he decided he would go and retrieve the company's Guinness. Accompanied by a driver's mate, he took a lorry to Hessle to try and find the wagon in which the casks were lying. They were stopped by strike pickets, who tried to turn them back. Charles was determined to press on and it looked as though the situation could turn ugly. He then had a brain wave and said, 'We are coming to pick up beer. If you stop us going through there will be nothing to drink in the clubs this weekend.' A big six-foot chap who seemed to be the spokesman said, 'You're going for the beer? Why didn't you say so before? Let them through.'

During the period after the First World War Jack faced a setback to his fortunes, which at the time seemed as though it would put the business at risk. As the firm had grown and prospered Jack had generated spare resources, which he had invested in a fishing company together with a number of other prominent local people. He was persuaded to sign a personal guarantee with the other directors. He thought that, if the company collapsed, he would only be called on to pay his share of the liability of a joint guarantee. In fact, he had signed a Joint and Several guarantee, which meant he could be called on to pay the lot. By the time he realised what he had done, the fishing company was in difficulty.

Jack was strongly advised by his solicitor and accountant that he should turn Faloon's and Townend's into private limited companies, in which he only had a minority shareholding, to protect his assets. In a way this problem was a blessing in disguise. Jack's personality would very likely have resulted in the business staying in his sole name and then having to be sold to pay death duties. Jack accepted this advice and in May 1923 a meeting of the promoters was held, which resolved that a private company be formed for the purpose of taking over as a going concern the business of wholesale and retail ale, porter, wine and spirit merchants carried out by Mr. J. Townend Snr. at 221 Beverley Road, Hull, and also the whole of the real and personal property of Mr. J. Townend Snr. The authorised share capital was to be £4,000. £3,900 £1 shares were issued to J. Townend in consideration for the following assets:

£	
1180	221 Beverley Road, Hull
600	4/6 Cave Street, Hull
800	4 cottages and blacksmith shop and land situated in Park Lane, Hull
430	Stepney Bowling Club
400	Bannister St., Withernsea
400	St. Helier Road, Cleethorpes
90	For goodwill, fixtures, fittings less bank overdraft

Total £3,900

Ten £1 shares were issued each to Mrs. Alice Townend, Mr. J. Townend Jnr and Mr. C. H. Townend. 70 shares were left unissued. Mr. J. Townend Snr then transferred shares so that the shareholding of the new company was as follows:

£	
900	J. Townend Snr.
610	C. H. Townend
610	J. Townend Jnr
610	Mrs. A. Townend
600	Miss A. Townend
600	Miss Annie Townend

Total £3,930

The first directors were J. Townend Snr, J. Townend Jnr, C. H. Townend and Mrs. A. Townend.

Why did Jack put all the property including that occupied by Faloon's into J. Townend & Sons (Hull) Limited? He was always a very shrewd man and perhaps he had already realised his assets would be safer in a company run by Charles than a company run by Jack Jnr. The records of the flotation of Faloon & Co. Ltd. have not survived but the twins were given the same amount of shares. The seeds of future problems were sown, for as the wine business went from strength to strength and Charles only had 15% of the shares, Faloon's started to decline and Charles saw the value of his holding fall.

Charles' marriage was quickly followed by that of his twin brother, who married Lillian Turner. Sister Annie (Nan), who worked in the office for Charles, in 1927 married Clive Rufford, the youngest son of George Rufford, another successful local businessman who operated a large draper's and furniture store in Fountain Road off Beverley Road. Alice, the elder daughter, then married Harold Johnson, the son of a local builder whose business unfortunately didn't survive the Depression.

The wine business outgrew the rear of Beverley Road so, whilst the office, in which Charles' sister Nan was now employed, remained in Beverley Road, the bottling moved to premises owned by Jack either at 4/6 Cave Street or Park Lane. In the late 1920s it was decided to demolish the old buildings in Cave Street and build a new building that would accommodate Townend's and also provide accommodation for Faloon's. It is known that prior to completion of the new building, Townend's bottling store was on the ground floor of the building in which the Park Lane Club was situated on the first floor. Ken Wood, who joined Charles in 1930 as a young boy from school and eventually rose to the position of General Manager, recalled that it was a dark, damp, windowless place and, when he was sitting on a box bottling by hand, it often happened that the beer pumps in the club upstairs would overflow and he would be showered with beer coming through the ceiling.

Hand bottling was pretty primitive. The wine flowed direct from the cask through a pipe into a silver-plated six-head rotating tap, which looked like a cow's udders. Empty bottles were placed on these pipes and they filled in turn. When a bottle was full, the operator took the full bottle off the tap, put a cork in it and placed it in a case. He then replaced the full bottle with an empty one. When he had finished bottling he would put a capsule over the cork and then label each bottle by hand and finally put it in a case, ready for delivery. A candle was often used to check that the wine coming off the bottler was clear.

The architects for the new building were a firm called Dosser's and it was with this firm that Alec, the youngest son, was training to be an architect. Townend's moved into the new building in Cave Street in the autumn of 1930. Faloon's lorry was borrowed to transfer the casks from Park Lane. The new bottling store was on the first floor, which had been built with very large strong wooden beams to take the weight of the casks, which had to be hoisted up on an outside hoist. On the ground floor, Townend's' office was on one side of the archway and Faloon's on the other side. Stock other than casks had to be carried through the offices and up the stairs.

Staff now consisted of Charles, a lady in the office, one older man and Ken Wood, a boy who did the bottling and packing. Because there was virtually no machinery, bottling was very slow; bottling stock for Christmas started in September. Overtime in the evening was 6-10 p.m., worked every night, and the staff were paid 2s 6d per evening (12½p). When Charles and Dorothy went to live in Bridlington in 1935 they used to rent a house in St. Hilda Street off Beverley Road for three months before Christmas because Charles worked every night until well after 10 p.m.

In the late 1920s there started a progressive decrease of the free trade as the brewers bought up free houses. They tied clubs to the brewery by making loans or buying the property. Jack himself in 1924 bought the property occupied by the Fountain Villa Club in Cholmley Street, Hull. Charles felt that to safeguard the future the company should build up a retail chain.

Spare hand bottling 1937.

Ken Wood on the box bike. *The Company's transport in the early 1930s* *The old van.*

Old warehouse and offices built in Cave Street, 1927. *Alec Townend, Charles Townend and Ken Wood, 1932.*

Chapter 3:

The 1930s

The 1930s was a period of considerable activity. In early 1930 the Company made the first of its many acquisitions. It purchased the old established business of J. J. Rippon founded in 1840 from Mrs. Margaret Rippon for £750, including Stock £445, Goodwill £100 and Fixtures £125.

Entry in *Industries of Yorkshire* (1890)
J. J. RIPPON, WINE AND SPIRIT MERCHANT
'Central Wine and Spirit Stores, Prospect Street (corner of Spring Bank), Hull – This large and influential business was established over fifty years ago. The premises in Prospect Street occupy a commanding position at the corner of Spring Bank. On the ground floor is a large and well appointed suite of offices, also sale and sample room; the premises likewise contain exclusive cellarage accommodation, bottling stores, fitted with the most approved appliances for bottling, corking, wiring, bottle washing, etc.

Mr. Rippon holds a very large and comprehensive stock of wines and spirits, ale, beer, and stout, liqueurs, mineral and aerated waters, etc., including some rare vintages, very fine old brandy, Scotch and Irish whisky, rum, gin, and liqueurs from the leading English, Scotch, Irish and Continental distilleries.

Amongst the specialities may be mentioned a very fine brand of Highland whisky, favourably known as the 'Dalmeny'. This well-known brand is steadily increasing in public favour and can with confidence be recommended.'

At the time of the takeover J. J. Rippon was situated in an old furniture store in Prospect Street next to the Central Cinema. Assets acquired included the trademark for 'Dalmeny' whisky and an old Morris van described by Ken Wood 'as having no starter'. It could only be started by swinging the starting handle. There was a piece of wire running under the bonnet for the choke and no wind-up window, just a door and side curtains. Townend's transport fleet now consisted of this old van and a three-wheeled box bike. Dalmeny Whisky became an important brand for Townend's after the war.

The manager of Rippon's was a wonderful character called Ezra Cade. He had been in the trade all his life and was very knowledgeable about fine wines. He was stooped with a fine head of white hair. He guarded his wines jealously, as was illustrated when Dorothy, Charles' wife, went to help out in the busy Christmas period. Mr. Cade went out for lunch and Dorothy, looking for something to do, saw a pile of bottles laid down, covered with dust and dirt. She decided they needed a good clean so she set to, picked them up one by one, dusting them, polishing them and then laying them down again. When he returned Ezra nearly had a heart attack because the bottles were vintage port and she had disturbed the crusts by moving them. 'What on earth will the customers think?' he said as he threw a shovel of dust and dirt all over the bottles to try and make them look as though they hadn't been touched for years.

Dorothy also tells of an old doctor called Dowsing, who recommended any patient suffering from cold or flu, to go to Rippon's and buy a bottle of Dalmeny. He said it was the best medicine there was.

In April 1934, the firm obtained its first on-licence premises when it took a 10-year lease on the Nag's Head Inn, Routh, from the Samman Estate at a rent of £50 a year. In 1938 the Estate was put on the market and was sold by auction. The directors decided to bid for it, they were successful and purchased the public house and an adjoining 12 acres of grassland. Harold Johnson's father's business had closed down, and, in order to help his daughter Alice, Jack made her the manageress, with her husband helping her during the evening when he came home from working as a builder. A second public house purchased in late 1938, was the Bull Inn at Gristhorpe, near Filey, for a figure of £1,200. Two more country public houses were acquired during the 1940s in North Yorkshire – the White Horse Norton, and the Grey Horse, Great Edston.

Following the acquisition of J. J. Rippon, there was a flurry of activity on the retail front. In February 1934 the Company rented a shop at Scunthorpe, but it did not trade profitably and after a couple of years was closed down. Interestingly enough the company went back to Scunthorpe during the 1960s and did very well. On 9 January 1936 the Minute Book records that the company took over the business of Thomas Tasker, wine merchant of 30-32 Cliff Street, Bridlington, for £2,500 including the property.

The next acquisition in 1936 followed the break up of Brown, Walker and Atkin, a very well respected firm at that time which had been formed by the amalgamation in 1897 of the two old businesses of Keyworth Walker & Co. and Hodgson, Gibson and Brown. There are two very interesting entries in books in the Hull library:

Pre-war retail branch, Cliff Street, Bridlington.

Messrs. Keyworth, Walker, & Co., Importers of Wines and Spirits: entry in *Modern Hull* (1893).

'Of over a century's standing, the business of Messrs. Keyworth, Walker, & Co., importers of Wines and Spirits, can claim to rank among the most substantial concerns in this particular line in the Port of Hull. Founded in the latter half of the last century, the business was first commenced by a Mr. Hannath, by whom it was continued for some years, and subsequently transferred to Messrs. Freshney & Keyworth. In course of time the title was again altered to T. Keyworth & Co., and in 1885, the firm was reconstituted as above indicated, the present partners comprising Mr. H. J. Walker and Mr. J. G. Atkin. The business headquarters of the firm is situated at No.11 King Street. The firm have also large warehouse in Parliament Street, branch wholesale and retail stores at the Old Corn Exchange, North Church Side, and private bonded stores in Posterngate. 'Their connection is very widespread, three travellers being employed in waiting upon customers, principally among hotel proprietors and private families in Yorkshire, Lincolnshire, Notts, Derby, and a part of Lancashire. As one of the oldest firms in the wine and spirit trade in the East Riding, Messrs. Keyworth, Walker, & Co. control a very large and important business and have secured the influential support which has so long been extended to this time honoured establishment.'

Hodgson, Gibson & Brown, Wine and Spirit Importers, 21 High Street, Hull published in *Industries of Yorkshire* (1890).

'This important business dates its history from the year 1827, when it was founded at its present headquarters in High Street, under the style of Hodgson, Gibson & Co. Exactly fifty years later (in 1877) the title was changed to its present form of Hodgson, Gibson & Brown, and the sole proprietor of the house is now Mr. William Kirk Brown.

The business has steadily advanced. The premises' offices, with wine cellars and stores in connection, and there is also a large bonded store of three flats, with every appliance for blending and vatting whiskies and rums. The blending vat here has a capacity of 800 gallons, and in it have been prepared for the market many of the superior brands of spirituous liquors for which this house is noted. This felicitous blend of noted Highland and Lowland distilleries is thoroughly matured in sherry casks.

As well as being wine merchants, Brown, Walker and Atkin owned a number of public houses including the historic 'Ye Olde White Hart'. It was in the plotting parlour of this Inn on the 23 April 1642 that John Hotham, Governor of Hull, his son, 2 Hull M.P.s and representatives of the town plotted to close the City gates against Charles I during the Civil War.'

In 1936 William Younger, the Scottish Brewers, acquired the business to obtain the public houses, but they didn't wish to get involved in the wine business. Because Faloon's bottled Younger beers they approached Townend's, who agreed to take the wine business over. It is recorded in the Minute Book: 'The company took over the premises of North Church side, adjacent to Holy Trinity, which consisted of office, shop and warehouses and premises in Beverley.' We believe that the latter were probably the refreshment rooms on Beverley Railway Station, now the excellent restaurant, Cerutti '2'. The purchase price was £3,874. The shop continued to operate until the war but the office and warehouse were closed down and two of the staff were transferred to Cave Street. Bob Stubbings had worked in the warehouse and he now joined Sid Curtis at the bottling store in Cave Street. Sid had joined as a young delivery boy at the Beverley Road shop and when Ken Wood moved into the office he took his place in the stores. Ken and Bob ran the stores until the outbreak of war. When they were bottling for Christmas Charles and Ken would give them a hand. The other member of the Brown, Walker staff to stay was a clerk called Donald Smith, who amongst his many jobs did the Bond papers. Apart from war service he stayed with Townend's until his retirement in the 1980s, after 40 years of service.

It was with this takeover that the Company started buying goods into Bond. The Company took over the small Brown, Walker Bond but HM Customs closed it down because it was considered by them to be too small to be economic, for in those days, whenever the Bond was open, a Customs Office had to be present. The Company was able to rent part of the Hull Brewery Bond in High Street and stayed there until they acquired their own Bond in York Street.

In June 1937, the company acquired a wine and spirit off-licence at 114 Spring Bank, Hull. This was managed by Billie and Harriet Irwin. Harriet was another niece of the alderman, as he was now known.

Charles Townend tasting wine, 1937.

In 1937 the company acquired yet another business, from Mr. A. Todd, 31 Queen Street, Withernsea, for £2,600 including the freehold property. Another outlet was acquired during this period, at Kingston Road, Willerby, where Jack Snr bought a shop and leased it to the company, which applied and obtained a new off-licence in 1938. The Minute Book shows two more financial investments, a second mortgage of £200 to Mr. P. Bray of the Marlborough Club, Hessle. Mr. Bray was married to one of Jack's nieces and no doubt in return for the loan the company obtained the trade.

During the 30s Alec Townend, the youngest son, joined the family firm. Jack Snr had never intended him going into the business. He had a better education than his brothers and sisters and had attended Hymers College, a day public school. He was destined to go into a profession rather than into 'trade'. He was articled to Dosser's the architects, who had built the Cave Street premises. As a schoolboy he had been rather cocky and his brothers commented that when he came onto the Cave Street site as a trainee architect he acted in a most superior way. He hated studying and, when the time had come for him to take his architectural examinations, he refused to take them and walked out of the practice. He thought he would walk straight into the business, but he got a rude awakening. His father was furious and refused to give him a job. As the youngest he was his mother's favourite and so for six months he had no job but he lived at home, his mother giving him pocket money and allowing him to drive around in her car. All the while, Alice was nattering at Jack to take him into the business. Eventually he gave in to get some peace. Alec wanted to work with Charles in the wine business but Charles said the business wasn't big enough so he joined Jack Jnr in Faloon's. It was Jack's biggest mistake because it caused the break-up of the family after his death. Jack would never allow him to be made a director during his lifetime and he didn't have any shares in the company until 1945 when he was allowed to buy the 70 unissued shares at par.

Joint staff dance at the Metropole, 1939 – Faloon's and Townend's.

Chapter 4:

The War 1939-1945

During the heavy bombing of Hull in 1941, Kingston Villa, Jack's residence, was badly damaged so Jack, who was now 68, decided to take his wife to live in an hotel at Windermere in the Lake District, leaving Charles to manage Townend's and Jack Jnr to run Faloon's. He still retained the title of Chairman and Managing Director of both companies, but the twins were now the *de facto* Managing Directors.

It was very difficult for small companies like Townend's to survive the war. Nearly all the men joined the Forces: Bob Stubbings, Ken Wood, Donald Smith, Sid Curtis, Fred Hancock and eventually Gordon Claire, together with several of the shop managers. Charles and Jack, having served in the First World War, were just too old. Alec failed his medical as he suffered from colitis. The firm was kept going by old men and women. The shop at Church Side was shut down in 1940 and the following year J. J. Ripon was closed only weeks before it was hit by a bomb. This was very fortunate because the stocks taken out of these two branches were invaluable in keeping the rest of the business supplied. Ezra Cade, who was well past normal retirement age, moved to Cave Street and ran the warehouse until the men came back after the war. When the first lot of men were called up, Gordon Clare, who was too young for the Forces, was moved from Beverley Road to help Mr. Cade in the stores until he was eventually called up in 1943.

One of the major problems during the War was getting hold of stock to sell. You could virtually sell anything. After 1940 imports were virtually non-existent so one had to rely on stocks in the U.K. Fortunately, in those days the British had a long tradition of buying wines when they were young and laying them down in the UK to mature. There were, therefore, a number of years' stock of good table wine such as Bordeaux, Burgundy and Vintage Port in the country. Gin, whisky and beer were on allocation, which was based on pre-War sales. Charles used to say that, during the War, if you had a bottle of whisky you could get anything.

Charles showed a great deal of initiative in obtaining stock. He travelled all over to buy virtually any liquor he could lay his hands on. He was helped very much by his friend Louis Porter, of Gale Lister. Being a wholesaler and retailer he could sell profitably through his retail branches anything he acquired. Because of the problems of getting petrol for the delivery vehicles it obviously was advantageous to put as much stock through the Beverley Road branch as possible as it could be taken by barrow from the warehouse in Cave Street, 20 yards down into the shop. As a result Beverley Road became one of the best wine and spirit shops in Hull because it had the reputation of never being out of stock.

As well as working during the day there was fire watching to be done at night. Hull was very badly bombed and in two nights in 1941 the whole of the centre of the city was flattened. Gordon Clare recalls that not only did he spend many sleepless nights fire fighting at Townend's premises during the bombing, his home was also bombed out. Despite the blitz he remembers that all work started at the normal time the next morning. The Cave Street premises managed to avoid being hit but John well remembers his father coming home one morning very upset; it was the night the Luftwaffe obliterated much of Cave Street and Charles had had the horrific task of helping the emergency services to pull dead and dying out of the rubble, many of whom he knew personally. Charles also spent much of his spare time with the Air Training Corps. In order to cope with these commitments he couldn't leave until after the last train to Bridlington had left so the family moved back from Bridlington and rented a house in Newland Park for the duration of hostilities.

After the First World War Charles had continued flying privately for a short time but he was not well paid by his father and so couldn't afford to continue the heavy cost. With the rise of Hitler in the 1930s the powers that be started to prepare for war. Air power was clearly going to be much more important than in the 1914-18 war and in the event at the Battle of Britain it was the difference between defeat and victory. In the late 1930s the ADCC (Air Defence Cadet Corps) was founded to train young men prior to them being called up to serve in the R.A.F.

A squadron was formed in Hull, the 152 City of Hull Squadron. It was natural that Charles as a former RFC pilot should become involved. The CO was Roy Croskin, who had been a keen private flier but who had no RAF experience. Charles was appointed Second in Command with the rank of Flight Lieutenant. As the organisation increased, more squadrons were established and Roy Croskin became the Wing Commander of the whole wing, Charles being promoted to Squadron Leader of the 152 Squadron. As so often with the Townend family, one in all in. Jack Townend became the Chairman of the Civilian Committee, Alec became the CO of the 192 Squadron and Jack Jnr was the Welfare Officer. Dorothy, who was already in the WVS, took over the running of the canteen with many of the young WVS girls. At the end of the war all the squadrons were disbanded with the exception of 152 Squadron. All the family retired with the exception of Jack Jnr, who became CO of the one remaining squadron.

During the War from 1942 onwards due to Charles' efforts Townend's made very good profits. He managed to keep the flow of goods coming in and there were very few staff to pay. Faloon's should also have done well but the decline that had started in the late 30s continued. Much of this was due to inefficiency. Charles used to say that at times there were so many leaks on the bottling machine that all the profit was going down the sink. A comparison of the two companies' profit performance is enlightening

	Faloon's		*Townend's*	
1938	£56	Profit	£280	Loss
1939	£335	Profit	£98	Profit
1940	£102	Loss	£36	Loss
1941	£1,007	Loss	£169	Profit
1942	£495	Profit	£2,569	Profit
1943	No record		£6,608	Profit
1944	£1,293	Profit	£8,500	Profit
1945	£1,235	Loss	£9,500	Profit
1946	£2,272	Loss	£8,900	Profit
1947	£2,440	Profit	£9,900	Profit
1948	£507	Loss	£11,800	Profit

Despite the disparate performance of the two companies, because they were twins, Jack Snr decreed that the two brothers should get the same salaries. This caused great resentment on the part of Charles.

Chapter 5:

Post-War Period 1945-59

Jack Townend had returned from Windermere in 1944 and immediately started going to Townend's office in Cave Street every day. Faloon's had moved out of Cave Street, leaving it completely occupied by Townend's, and now had its office in Park Lane adjacent to the beer bottling plant. When Faloon's started to decline Jack refused to even go into their offices. 'It is a mess pot,' he would say and would not exercise his powers as Chairman to take any action. To be fair, he was well into his seventies by this time. His daily routine was to rise about nine, have a breakfast cooked by his wife, which usually included two lamb chops, and, because he had never learnt to drive, he would then be collected by his driver and driven to Charles' office, arriving around 10.30. He would call for a bottle of whisky from stock and start drinking it. He would offer anyone who came to see him a glass of whisky and he would not go home until the bottle was finished. The time he was taken home depended on the number of visitors he had, as did his sobriety.

Having been left to get on with running the business on his own since 1939 Charles didn't take kindly to his father getting under his feet. If he had gone to Faloon's office 2½ days a week he would perhaps have accepted the situation better. It was about this time that his old friend Louis Porter of Gale Lister suggested that Charles leave his father and go and live in Leeds and work for him. In view of the fact that Louis Porter died within a few years, it was a good job that he resisted this tempting offer.

Charles' son John was a pupil at Hymers College by this time, and recalls that from time to time he would walk from the College to his father's office to be taken home in the car. On these occasions he would sit and talk to his grandfather. Jack had ten grandchildren, five boys and five girls, and, as John was the only one who played rugby, he was his grandfather's favourite. Grandpa gave all his family, including grandchildren and in-laws, £1 each for Christmas and £1 each for birthdays. On one occasion out of the blue Grandpa asked John what he would like for his birthday. John replied he would like a pair of new tennis shorts. 'How much will they cost?' asked Grandpa. 'I don't know,' said John. Grandpa said, 'I will buy them but your mother will have to go and get them and I will give her the cost.' John's mother couldn't believe it when John told her. However, she went and bought them for £3 and grandpa paid up. This was the only time he ever deviated from his standard £1.

Grandpa, to Dorothy's annoyance, used to call John, Jack. Dorothy told her son not to answer to Jack and when Grandpa complained that John was ignoring him she replied, 'He will only answer to his proper name, John.' Grandfather then said to John, 'You should like to be called Jack Townend and then when you grow up people will say are you related to "the Jack Townend".' These were the words of a man who clearly thought he had achieved something in his lifetime.

On another occasion he asked John what he was going to do when he left school. John was very much influenced by his mother at the time and, because of the problems her husband had had, she was determined he would have a profession. When someone had told him as a young child that a solicitor received 7s 6d every time anyone rang him up, John decided he wanted to be a solicitor. So he replied to his grandfather's question, 'I want to be a lawyer.' 'You don't want to be a lawyer,' said Jack. 'Lawyers are all liars. You go and be an accountant and then you can come and work for me and be of some use.' 'Work for you, Grandpa, and have you treat me like you have treated my father, no way,' said John (repeating his mother's views). 'I wouldn't treat you like your father,' said Grandpa. 'I wouldn't get away with it with you,' he said with a twinkle in his eye. 'You are too like me.' When John reported this to his mother she wasn't amused.

The immediate post-war period was quite difficult. Business had shrunk due to shortages, and suddenly there was a great influx of staff who had been demobilised from the Forces. Wood, Claire, Smith, Hancock, Curtis all returned but Bob Stubbins seems to have got employment elsewhere. Because of the large scale destruction of the City of Hull during the Blitz, firms within the Hull boundary became subject to a statutory licensed planning scheme, which prevented anyone opening a new wine shop in the City unless they had been allocated an opportunity through the scheme. Opportunities were allocated on the basis of bombed property. As the brewers had lost a large number of worthless backstreet shops they got the lion's share of the allocation and because Townend's had vacated J. J. Rippon before it was bombed, they got none. This made it virtually impossible to expand in Hull.

One area that the Company did develop was the operation of licensed bars at dances, weddings and functions by means of an occasional licence. This required the use of an On Licence. In the early days the licence of the Beverley Refreshment Rooms was used and the steward of the Fountain Villa Club ran the bars. When he left, Ken Wood took over and he was most successful. The firm co-operated closely with a Leeds firm of caterers who had no licensed side, so Townend's provided the bar service for all these functions. It was a Jewish firm and their main clients were from the wealthy Leeds Jewish community, who entertained quite royally for weddings, Bar Mitzvahs and other celebrations.

Walter Redhead, a wonderful character who joined the firm in the late 40s, had a fund of stories about these events. Many of the guests had a taste for strange and exotic drinks, particularly one called 'Bloodshot Eyes', which consisted of an advocaat with a shot of cherry brandy.

On 23 September 1948 Jack Townend and his wife celebrated their Golden Wedding with a dinner dance held at the Blind Institute, Beverley Road, Hull. It was a happy event for they were surrounded by their five children, in-laws, ten grandchildren and many friends. There were, of course, lots of speeches as is normal at such functions and John recalls that at the time he was quite a precocious 14-year-old and, as the eldest Townend grandson, volunteered to speak on behalf of the other grandchildren. However, family jealousies reared their heads, not for the first time, and Maureen, the eldest of the grandchildren, who had no wish whatsoever to speak, was dragooned by her mother into making the speech.

Just over a year later, on 22 December 1949, Alderman Jack Townend died, aged 78. When the founder of a company, who still holds the office of Chairman and Managing Director dies, it is certainly the end of an era. Jack's achievements had been considerable. He started from humble beginnings and created two successful businesses. He became an Alderman and was both popular and respected. He had a wonderful life, which he enjoyed to the full; he was a fine sportsman and somewhat of a *bon-viveur*. He had a way with people that usually got them to do what he wanted. He never retired, but did practically no work for his last 25 years. Despite his working-class origins, he was a lifelong Tory and, like so many successful entrepreneurs, he was a character, somewhat larger than life. However, he did not leave a happy situation. Faloon's was rapidly going downhill and Charles was left a minority shareholder in Townend's, at the mercy of his siblings.

After the reading of the will, an Extraordinary General Meeting was held to confirm the appointment of Charles, the eldest son, as Chairman and Managing Director of J Townend & Sons (Hull) Limited. He had been the *de facto* MD for some years, he was now in charge but not in control and he had to wait until the start of the next decade to achieve this lifelong ambition.

When Charles, the second generation, took over, wartime restrictions and rationing had not yet disappeared and business was difficult. As the Company was not able to expand its retail chain of five branches, Charles concentrated on establishing brands which would hopefully be sold to the wholesale trade. He established the Red Duster brand for rum and dealt in large quantities of bulk rum. He blended the rum himself at the stores in Cave Street. The rum had to be broken down – that is reduced in strength by the addition of distilled water prior to bottling. When one did this one couldn't help inhaling the fumes of the over-proofed rum. Charles often had to go and lie down after completing the operation because he was somewhat drunk from the fumes despite never a drop passing his lips. His long-term competitor for rum was Moor's and Robson's, the local brewery whose rum brand was Lord Charles. Because of the financial clout of a brewery company in the Club trade, Lord Charles always outsold Red Duster.

Townend's had inherited the Dalmeny whisky brand from J. J. Rippon in 1930. In the pre-war period they used to buy small casks of blended whisky, which was bottled by hand. During the war it was impossible to buy bulk whisky, so the brand disappeared from the market. After the war, when it became possible to buy bulk whisky again, Charles decided to re-launch the Dalmeny brand. He always made quality one of his most important requirements and he was determined to make Dalmeny whisky of a superior quality to ordinary proprietary brands, such as Haig, Johnny Walker and Dewar's. Because Scotch whisky needs to mature for a number of years in casks, he had to start by buying bulk-blended whisky, which was over three years old and could be bottled immediately. He then had to fill individual whiskies, which would be brought down from the distillery, immediately after they had been produced, to the Bond in Scarborough.

His first blend contained good quality malts, such as Highland Park, Glen Rothies and Tamdhu and the grain was the Number One from North British. The very top malts were very difficult to obtain, because the demand was greater than the supply. Over the years Charles, with the help of Frank Roughsedge, Chairman of Hall & Bramley, was able to get allocations from the top distillers, such as Glen Grant, Smith's Glenlivet and Longmorn. As a result, the quality progressively improved.

There are three methods of producing high quality blend:

1. Use top-class whiskies.
2. Put a higher proportion of malt in the blend than the normal brands.
3. Mature the whisky for more than four years, rather then the standard three-year blend.

When the single whiskies were matured, the casks were then transferred to the York Street Bond, where they were blended and reduced to a strength of 70% proof, and bottled. The quality was excellent and the Company built up a small but loyal band of customers who appreciated quality more than the label or the price.

Charles also launched a range of sherry under the Kingston label and was very proud of the quality of these brands, especially the Kingston Cream. This was an elegant sweet Olorosso, lighter than the Bristol Cream style, which was very sweet and cloying. When Harvey's advertised Bristol Cream as 'the best Sherry in the world', Charles got very annoyed, saying his Kingston Cream was better.

A pioneering brand launched in 1955 was Baby Cherry. This was the first cherry wine bottled in small Babycham sized bottles. The main outlets were public houses and clubs, where it was mainly drunk by women as an alternative to the increasingly dated port and lemon. Charles himself got a number of good customers, including Hewitt's Brewery in Grimsby, who took a weekly order of at least 100 cases. Ken Wood was also sent out selling but didn't like it and Charles made a big mistake in not appointing a full-time experienced salesman. In 1956 the sales were 5,820 cases, rising to 23,063 the following year.

Unfortunately, the bulk wine for this brand was manufactured by Vine Products, a large national company, and, when they saw the success that Baby Cherry was having in a limited area, they launched a national brand, Cherry B, with a large advertising budget and blew Baby Cherry out of the water. It was not to be the first time that the big battalions beat the Townend's small family company.

Bottling cellars, Cave Street, early 1960s.

Charles had always felt the name J Townend & Sons (Hull) Limited was rather a mouthful and did not look particularly good on shop fronts. He decided to change the trading name to The House of Townend. To market the rebranding he advertised The House of Townend as Hull's leading wine merchants. This caused some resentment in the trade because at that time Townend's were not considered to have acquired such status. It is interesting to note that all the Hull wine merchants of that era – Hull Brewery, Lambert Parker & Gaines, Southam's, Henry Wilson, Wild's, Ruddock's, Evelyn Cooke and Moor's & Robson's have all ceased to exist.

In 1954 the Company acquired Marks, 99 Osborne Street, which was a small run-down wine shop whose only claim to fame was that, due to its Jewish owner, it was considered the only place to buy Kosher wines. The shop was just outside the central area and it was purchased with a view to transferring the licence and business into a busy shopping street. In the same year the Company terminated the tenancy at the Nag's Head in order to modernise it and put it under management. This meant that the licence could be used for catering licences for the outside bar catering department. The loss making refreshment rooms at the Beverley railway station, whose licence had been previously used, were no longer necessary and the lease was surrendered.

After Alderman Jack's death, Jack Jnr was appointed Chairman and Managing Director of Faloon & Co. and Alec was appointed a director. During the last years of their father's life they had been in management control but they had failed to make a success of the business. Growing losses made it increasingly clear that the company could not survive under the management of Jack and Alec. There was no alternative but to cede control. The controlling interest, therefore, was sold to William Younger in about 1952. The family sold the balance of the shares to Scottish Brewers, the successors to William Youngers, in 1960. This was a bitter blow to the family as beer bottling and wholesaling had been the original basis of Alderman Jack's fortune. As part of the deal, Townend's granted a 99-year lease, together with an Option to Purchase, to Faloon & Co., who were occupying the Park Lane premises owned by Townend's.

The Scottish Brewers exercised this Option to Purchase in 1962. Subsequently, Scottish Brewers closed down their Hull depot and the site was redeveloped for housing; the considerable profits, of course, went to the brewery company, not to the original owners.

In 1955 Charles made one of his greatest mistakes when he was persuaded to sell three of the four pubs – the Grey Horse at Great Edston, the Bull Inn at Gristhorpe and the White Horse at Beadlom to Faloon's, which was now controlled by Youngers. The price for all three was £3,500. Even allowing for the large change in the value of money, it was a ridiculously low price. Part of the deal was that Townend's would supply all their requirements for wines and spirits in perpetuity, or so Charles believed. Townend's were also supplying a number of other Youngers' pubs in the area, including the well-known George and Dragon at Aldbrough. A few years later Scottish Brewers started their own wine and spirit subsidiary and Townend's lost the trade, including that of the three pubs they had sold. Charles discovered to his chagrin that the supply deal was not as watertight as he had thought and was not in perpetuity.

Chapter 6:

The Battle for Control

When Jack died in 1949 he left his 900 shares to his sons. 400 each to the twins and 100 to Alec, the youngest son. This meant that Charles and Jack Jnr controlled more than 50% of the shares. The shareholdings were:

Charles	1,010
Jack Townend Jnr	1,010
Mrs. A. Townend	610
Alec Townend	170
Miss Johnson	600
Nan Rufford	600
Total	**4,000**

Charles had become Chairman and Managing Director and, as a result of pressure from their mother and sisters, Charles and Jack agreed that Alec should be made a director. The combination of Jack's death and Alec being appointed a director began the process of the disintegration of the family, which had been kept together by their father. Perhaps he kept Alec off the Board in his lifetime because he had a premonition of what would happen.

As the financial position of Faloon's deteriorated, Charles became more and more worried about the future of Townend's. There was pressure by Jack and Alec for Townend's to guarantee Faloon's overdraft and Charles felt he would soon be faced by demands to amalgamate the two companies. His worry was that Faloon's would drag Townend's down to disaster. When Alice, their mother, died in 1955 she left all her shares to Alec as she had resented her husband's determination to keep his influence in the business to a minimum.

After his mother died Charles realised his position was becoming untenable, for he only owned 25.2% of the shares and on the Board he could be outvoted 2:1. He was only able to keep management control because the family needed his expertise. He was also helped very much by Eric Moss, the Company's auditor, who had a

wonderful way with words. Many is the time his soothing words at Board meetings prevented a blow-up and enabled Charles to maintain his position. Charles began to believe that the only way forward was to try and buy control of the Company. Jack and Alec were determined only to sell if the whole Company was sold. The alternative was for Charles to try and buy out his two sisters, Alice and Nan. Alice, whose husband's family business had gone to the wall in the recession, was always short of cash and was quite prepared to sell. Nan wouldn't sell because she thought it would let Alec down and she enjoyed the power that she had, because, as Alice would always support Charles against Jack and Alec, when the chips were down Nan had the decisive vote.

Charles' son, John, left school in 1951. He wanted to be a wine merchant but because of the family situation Charles, quite correctly, advised him not to go into the business but to go and qualify as a Chartered Accountant. John joined Smailes, Holtby and Gray, Chartered Accountants of 99 Princes Avenue, Hull. He signed five-year articles and worked as an audit clerk all day from 9 to 5.30 pm and studied for his examinations at night and during the weekends by means of a correspondence course. He still found time to play rugby for the Old Hymerians and represent the Cottingham Tennis Club in the local league, as well as taking an active interest in politics. He joined the Cottingham Young Conservatives at the age of 15 and by the time he was 17 he was the Chairman. He subsequently became the Divisional Chairman of the Haltemprice Constituency Young Conservatives and, when the boundaries changed, the Chairman of the Haltemprice and Beverley Young Conservatives. Despite leading an active sporting and social life he managed to gain the seventh place in the Institute of Chartered Accountants' Intermediate Examination and was awarded a Plender Prize for the best Paper in Advanced Accounting in his Finals.

As the only son, John knew all about the problems his father was facing with his brothers and he appreciated the only solution was to acquire 51% of the shares by hook or by crook. Even if his aunts were prepared to sell, his father would have to raise a considerable amount of money. As the years went by and the firm prospered and progressed the problem got worse because the value of the shares increased. Out of the blue Charles had a stroke of luck. In 1957 he got to know that an off-licence in Horsforth in the West Riding, near Leeds, was on the market – perhaps someone saw an advertisement in the *Yorkshire Post*. Ken Wood went to view it and found it was a very small shop and a very poor property in a back street between two roads. What excited him, however, were the sales, which were surprisingly high, and the asking price was very modest. The shop was owned and operated by Mrs. Hilda Keeling. It had been bought to keep her occupied by her husband, Eddie Keeling, a successful haulier. There was practically no competition and the suburb of Horsforth had expanded quickly and trade had grown. The price was modest because the Inland Revenue were investigating them and they wanted a quick sale. John saw this as a great opportunity and urged his father to purchase the business for himself, rather than for the company.

Initially Charles was reluctant because he feared upsetting the family but John, supported and urged on by Dorothy, his mother, managed to persuade his father into taking a chance. This was the first of many occasions on which the two of them combined. John argued that, as Townend's branches were restricted to the East Riding, a shop in West Yorkshire could not in the remotest way be said to be competing with J Townend & Sons. In addition, it would be a customer for Townend's, as they would purchase all their wines from the main company. John would keep the books in the evening and profits could be built up to provide cash for the future purchase of shares in Townend's. Charles finally agreed. The property, fixtures and business were acquired for only £3,500, with stock at valuation. A partnership, H. Keeling & Co., was set up consisting of Charles, Dorothy and John. It was decided not to form a separate company, so that Dorothy could get earned income as a partner. This was advantageous as far as taxation was concerned. However, this decision was to have a significant adverse effect on the family's future fortunes. Dorothy had inherited money from her father and she invested some of this in Keeling's. John had received modest legacies from both grandfathers, which he invested. Charles put up the rest of the money. The National Westminster Bank provided the overdraft facilities to finance the stock. It was at least a year before the family found out. Alec went mad but there was nothing he could do. Harold Crosby was appointed as manager and the whole project was a great success. Within three years profits were approximately £3,500 per year, or a 100% return on capital.

In 1960 a second shop was acquired, at 1 Albert Square, Yeadon, only four miles from the first shop. This was a licensed grocery. John joined the Spar organisation, as he had no knowledge of the grocery trade. Derek Johnson was appointed manager and for many years it was very profitable. Eventually the company decided the unit did not fit in with the company's image and it was sold to the manager, who was still Derek Johnson

John qualified as a Chartered Accountant, in 1957, and Charles thought his expertise would be helpful to the company and proposed he be appointed as a Director. Alec and Jack said they would agree but Charles would have to accept that Pat, Jack's eldest girl, and Colin, Alec's son, would also join the Board. This was despite the fact that neither of them had any expertise or training or, indeed, any interest, in the wine trade. Charles naturally would not agree, so there was a deadlock. Shortly afterwards, John went into the RAF to do his National Service. Showing his usual initiative he had discovered that one could apply for a commission before being called up. He applied and was asked to go for a selection weekend to RAF Uxbridge. He attended with about two dozen other candidates and six of them were selected, so he entered the RAF with the rank of Officer Cadet. After a few days at Cardington, where they were kitted out, on a miserable November day he embarked for the Officer Cadet Training Unit at Jurby in the Isle of Man. November, December and January is not the best time to be on the Island and John recalls that three days under canvass at the Point of Ayre in January, with winds so strong that the guy ropes were torn out of the tents, was something that he would not wish to repeat.

The situation suddenly changed when, unfortunately, Jack died from a heart attack in 1958. There was now a vacancy both for a Director and for the position of

Company Secretary, which Jack had held since the company was formed, although the work had been done by Eric Moss, the auditor. A Board Meeting was called for 11 March 1958. Those present were Charles Townend, Alec Townend and Eric Moss. The following extract from the Minutes gives a flavour of the events. It must be pointed out that C. H. Townend had made it clear that, if R. A. (Alec) Townend voted against John's appointment, he would use his casting vote.

Minutes

The Chairman said that it now became necessary to consider the appointment of a Director and Secretary to fill the vacancy caused by the death of Mr. Jack Townend.

The Chairman proposed that his son was a Chartered Accountant and had all those qualities necessary, including a knowledge of the Wine and Spirit Trade, to fill those positions, and moved that his son should be elected to the Board and to fill the position of Secretary.

Mr. R. A. Townend said that he agreed in principle, that Mr. J. E. Townend should come on to the Board, but that the Board should be extended to give another two seats. Mr. R. A. Townend went on to say further that he agreed that Mr. John Townend should be the Secretary, but in due course, when he came out of the Forces.

The Chairman disagreed. He said that the number of Directors was three, and always had been three, and that he saw no reason for extending the Board, and that there was no point in waiting until Mr. J. E. Townend came out of the Forces to be appointed the Secretary, since he could carry out and fulfil those duties during his leaves.

Mr. R. A. Townend said that he would carry out and fulfil the duties of Secretary for the time being. Mr. Charles Townend said that he considered that Mr. R. A. Townend's duties as Managing Director of Faloon & Co. Limited were so heavy that he could not, and indeed ought not, to consider an appointment as Secretary of J.

Townend & Sons (Hull) Limited. The Meeting then moved into a lengthy discussion on all points.

After some time, Mr. Moss intervened and proposed that it would perhaps be of assistance to clear the matter if each appointment was taken and dealt with separately.

In consequence, and after further length discussion, Mr. C. H. Townend again moved that his son, John Ernest Townend, be elected to the Board to fill the vacancy caused by the death of Mr. Jack. After some further discussion, Mr. R. A. Townend agreed, and Mr. J. E. Townend was duly elected to the Board.

Mr. Moss was instructed to prepare and lodge with the Registrar of Companies the necessary forms in relation to Mr. J. E. Townend's appointment.

Considerable discussion then ensued as to the proposed appointment of Mr. J. E. Townend to become the Secretary of the Company. Mr. R. A. Townend repeated that he thought it would be advisable to wait until Mr. John came out of the Forces, and suggested his own appointment as Secretary of the Company.

Mr. Charles Townend again pointed out the position with regard to Faloon & Co., Ltd., and suggested that the more appropriate appointment would be Mr. Ken Wood, the Manager of Townend's, as Secretary of the Company. Mr. R. A. Townend, however, opposed this.

After further discussion, Mr. Moss said that there appeared to be something of a deadlock and, in order that the parties could consider the position, he suggested that the appointment should be deferred. This was agreed, and that the matter should be brought up at the next Meeting of the Directors.'

Ken Wood was offered a good job by a wine merchant in Sutton Coldfield called Evenson. It was owned by Stuart Eve, who happened to be father of the famous actor, Trevor Eve. He operated a chain of shops in the

Birmingham area, so Ken accepted the appointment. Charles, now 60 years of age, was distraught and didn't know how he would manage. John managed to get posted to Topcliffe in Yorkshire and drove home every Wednesday evening to do the wages and then drove back at the crack of dawn to be on duty by 9 o'clock the next day.

With all the family being short of cash and Alec's position with Faloon's beginning to look more and more vulnerable, John felt there would be a growing danger that the company would be sold over Charles' head. He persuaded his father to make one more try to buy control. The alternatives were to buy the 1,200 shares owned equally by Nan and Alice or to buy out Jack's widow, Lilian, who held 1,010 shares. Charles' first preference was that his hard earned money should go to his sisters rather than his sister-in-law. Once more they approached the girls. Alice was prepared to sell but Nan, influenced by Alec, refused. That left only one option – Lilian. Charles was reluctant to approach her but the opportunity arose when it was announced that the younger daughter would shortly marry. Lilian wanted to give her a good wedding and it was known she was short of ready cash, so John thought that now was the time to strike. He persuaded his father to allow him to ring her and persuade her at least to have a discussion. In view of the animosity in the family and his father's feeling of resentment that he was going to have to pay heavily for the fruits of his labour, John knew it would be difficult to negotiate a deal without the balloon going up. His tactic, therefore, at the meeting was not to talk about price but to point out to Lilian the disadvantage of being a minority shareholder in a family business when you are not a member of the family and the advantage of having cash to spend or invest for a bigger return. He suggested that they wouldn't like to take advantage of her and that she should put the matter in the hands of her financial and legal advisers to negotiate with Charles' solicitor and accountant. To John's relief and surprise, she agreed. However, after all the professionals had met, Charles was horrified when it was reported that Lilian's advisers had said at the first meeting, 'We don't want to waste a lot of time negotiating.

We accept that, whether you value the shares on a break-up value or an asset value, or on the basis of the yield, it is impossible to justify a value of more than £10 for a £1 share. We want £15, £5 a share nuisance value.'

Charles' first reaction was anger and he said in no way was he going to pay through the nose for his own business and, in any case, he hadn't got the money. John had to persuade him that, whatever it cost, he had to get control if he wanted to ensure the survival of the business and the family. In the end they managed to settle for £12.50 per share, £2.50 nuisance value. Together with his own shares Charles and John now held 50.2% of the Company, just above the magic 50%.

John recalls the day the transfer was signed and exchanged for the cheque. A bottle of champagne was cracked to celebrate. Jennifer, his girlfriend and future wife, recalls that, when he picked her up from her home that evening to take her out on a date, she couldn't understand his excitement for she had know nothing of the delicate negotiations. That night John said he remembered the words of Churchill, the night he became Prime Minister. He said, and I quote, 'I slept soundly for the first time in months because I knew the country was in safe hands.' John now knew that the future of Townend's would end up in his hands. A Board meeting was swiftly called and on 29 April 1960 the transfer of Lilian's shares was registered. John recalls the look of astonishment on Alec's face, for he had thought he had persuaded all the females in the family to hang on to their shares. He knew the threat he posed to Charles and John had been smashed forever and they could now do what they wished. This power was used quickly. A meeting was called three weeks later, which strengthened their control and helped Charles and John finance the purchase.

Resolution 1: moved by Charles and seconded by John, that John be appointed Deputy Chairman and Deputy Managing Director, carried 2 votes to 1.

Resolution 2: proposed by John and seconded by Charles, that Charles' salary be increased by 50% to £3,000 p.a., carried 2 votes to 1.

Resolution 3: that J. Townend & Sons (Hull) Limited purchase John's MG car at the purchase price, which then became a company car for John's use, carried 2 votes to 1.

John said to his father that any future share purchases would now be fixed at £6 a share, take it or leave it.

There was a twist to the story because years later, when Nan Rufford died, her children did not want the shares and asked Bill Bowes, their solicitor, to try to sell them to John. He rang John, whom he knew quite well as they were both Governors of Hymers College. John offered £6 a share. He said, 'Come on John, you know that is much lower than what they are worth. Be a decent chap and give us a fair price.' John replied, 'Bill, do you recall when you acted for my late Aunt, you knew our shares were worth no more than £10, but you held a pistol to our head and we had to pay over the odds? This time I hold the cards and £6 is my price.' Three days later Bill Bowes rang back and accepted. This was the last block of shares held outside Charles' family. Alice had sold out some years before and Alec had pledged his shares to his bank to finance a business venture that went wrong. The bank had lent John the money to buy them and Alec had to resign from the Board.

Chapter 7:

The 1960s

In 1959 John joined the Company as Finance Director and Company Secretary after completing his National Service in the RAF. From his experience as an auditor, visiting family businesses, he was well aware of the problems that can often develop into wars between members of the family – in particular between father and son. He, therefore, said to his father that to avoid misunderstandings and problems they should consider each having properly designated responsibilities. John suggested that as he was a Chartered Accountant he should take charge of the office and accounts. He also wanted to expand the business, so he suggested he should be responsible for sales while his father, who had had many years of practical experience in the industry, should be responsible for the buying and the production and distribution. Charles, his father, refused point blank saying, 'I am the boss and I am in charge of everything,' and then within six months virtually stopped work! So John was thrown in at the deep end. He was young and ambitious and decided that the way to increase profits and expand the business was to increase the number of retail shops (then five) and establish Townend's as the leading retail chain in the region.

The Company had always worked on an overdraft and did not have unlimited resources to buy existing shops, which, because of licensing restrictions, fetched premium prices. John preferred to buy freehold but he hated paying large sums for goodwill. John set out a strategy for increasing the chain by getting options on freehold properties and applying for new off-licences. Because licence planning prevented new applications in Hull, initially John targeted the suburbs outside the city boundary, which were growing rapidly due to the ridiculous policy of the Labour-controlled Council to refuse planning consent for building private houses and only build massive council estates on the land available. Over time, John developed a formula that proved very successful. Having selected the target suburb or town he got a large-scale map, on which he marked all the licensed premises, one colour for On Licences and a different colour for Off Licences. Normally there would be no more than one or two Off Licences. He would draw two concentric circles from existing Off Licences, one of a quarter mile and one of half a mile. This map would, in due course, be presented to the magistrate as part of the case for the licence being granted. In those days, one had to prove the need for an additional licence and, therefore, the search for shop premises would, if possible, be outside the half-mile radius and it would certainly not be within the quarter mile radius.

John would then spend hours walking the areas that surrounded potential sites; his wife, Jennifer, remembers spending hours pushing the pram and taking the dog round Anlaby Common, which was near to where they lived, when he was looking for a site. Having identified the site, which might not be the best shopping site because of the need to be a fair way from existing facilities, the price had then to be negotiated and, if possible, the owner persuaded to grant a 'three-month option' to purchase, whilst the licence application was made.

To prove need, John used to lead a team of his staff knocking on doors, asking householders to sign a petition supporting the granting of a new licence. During this process he acquired the patter of the doorstep salesmen, which came in useful when he entered local politics and stood for election to Hull City Council. When there were existing Off Licences fairly near, he tried to get two or three business or professional people to go to court as witnesses to say there was a need for a new, specialist wine shop, which would supply a much better service and selection of wine than the local 'Offy'. John worked closely with a local solicitor, Lesley Davies, who from his working with Townend's subsequently became recognised as the leading licensing solicitor in the area. The system worked; on every occasion a licence was obtained. The first was South Ella in 1959, Cottingham 1961, Ferriby, Hornsea Caravan Park and Hessle in 1962, Anlaby in 1963 and Hedon in 1968. Having covered the Hull suburbs he then went further afield with

Post-war branch, Cottingham.

Scunthorpe in 1966 and Garforth and Selby in 1967.

The first Manager of Hessle was Harry Beacock. He was a wonderful character, who joined the army as a boy soldier and finished the war as a captain in what became the SAS. He eventually moved in 1967 to open the new Garforth branch, where he stayed until his retirement. If the new branch was opened in October or November it was found that the Christmas period was usually sufficient to provide a profit by the year end of 31 January. In the first full financial year a small profit would be made or break-even achieved so new branches were not a burden on the existing business.

Some existing businesses were purchased; H Keeling & Co. acquired a second branch in Yeadon in 1960 and a third branch in Bradford during 1964. Both were licensed grocers; the latter was not a great success and was disposed of in 1969. In the same year the Bridlington branch was closed, which illustrated that John was not afraid to close branches that were not performing. The licensed planning system came to an end and the Company was able to apply for licences in Hull. In 1969 it opened a branch in Bransholme.

John also refurbished the existing branches he had inherited; Beverley Road in 1959 and Kingston Road in 1961 were refurbished and the sales areas extended. In 1965 the little old shop in Osborne Street,

Hull, which was losing money, was closed and the licence transferred to a large city centre shop in Telephone House, Carr Lane.

John was always keen to be at the cutting edge of wine retailing and he decided upon the revolutionary idea of making this new city-centre shop into a self-service wine store. At that time self-service was just taking off in the United States and only a handful of grocery stores were trying it in the United Kingdom; supermarkets were still in the future at that time. John decided he needed advice in looking at an existing operation, so he contacted NCR, who supplied him with cash registers, and asked if there were any self-service specialist wine shops in the UK. To his surprise they wrote back and said they did not know of any but there was one in Dublin called Bacchus Wine owned by an interesting character Aiden Doyle. Through his contact with Jameson's, the Irish Whiskey

distillers in Dublin, he obtained an introduction to Aiden and flew over to Dublin to view this new store. What he saw confirmed his view that he should try and do something similar in England and he adapted what he had seen in Dublin to the premises in Carr Lane. Instead of trading as 'The House Of Townend' he called it the 'Wine Centre' with the slogan, 'All the world's wines'. When it opened it was a tremendous success, particularly during the festive period.

The meeting with Aiden proved to be significant for he introduced John to George Sère, a wine *négociant* and merchant from Lourdes. John accompanied Aiden on his next visit to France to see George, who was not in business in a big way but was excellent at blending wines and sniffing out good producers. He was also very well known and influential in the wine industry in south-west France. John started importing in bulk – Corbière, Madiran and Jurançon from George. These wines were little known in the UK at that time. The Madiran wine was of outstanding value, as long it was kept in bottle for two to three years. To John's surprise and delight, he received a telephone call one day from the Savoy hotel in London, enquiring about this wine, which had been tasted by one on their directors whilst lunching with a banker in Paris. They had contacted George, who referred them to his UK agent, John. This resulted in an annual order for 200 cases, which went on for years until George suddenly died and John was then unable to find a Madiran of the same quality.

John became very friendly with George and used to spend a week each year being taken around growers across the South West of France. George also used to visit or 'jump', in his words, England and Ireland every year. One day he telephoned John and said, 'You and Jennifer must "jump" to Dublin, for we have arranged "a Chapter of the Wine Brotherhood of Jurançon". I am coming over to preside and I would like to make you a Member.' John and Jennifer flew over and stayed at the Shelbourne Hotel, where the dinner was to take place. After the four new Members had been installed and robed, George suddenly said out of the blue, 'You will all have to make a speech.' Apart from John, the other three were the Head of the Irish Tourist Board, the

Managing Director of Gilbey's, Ireland – both Irish – and the Managing Director of Grants, Ireland, who was English. The Grant's man spoke first, to great applause, saying what a wonderful place Ireland was and that he had ceased to feel English a couple of weeks after disembarking. John was desperately searching round for something humorous to say as he was the second one called to speak. He suddenly had a brainwave. He rose and said, 'As my friend, Bernard, the Grant's man, no longer considers himself an Englishman, it would seem I am the only representative here tonight of your former colonial rulers' – and waited for the laugh. There was a deathly silence and then the two Frenchmen laughed politely while the Irish remained silent. John was clearly not politically correct, long before that phrase came into existence.

John believed that visiting the wine areas was imperative if one was to get the best quality wines at a good price. He took every opportunity he could, beginning with a visit to Portugal for the Vintage in 1962. In the early years of the Merchant Vintners, the bulk importers of the Group, Richard Tanner, John Moran and Derek Balls and John often travelled with one another. They learnt a lot from each other and, when buying, found that two tasters are often better than one. They introduced each other to their contacts. When Richard went on a trip to south-west France with John, he was surprised at the extent of his sources and contacts which he had got from George Sère. For a number of years, John went annually with Derek Balls to buy the Group's Beaujolais. This tradition of extensive travelling has been continued by John Charles, but now it is not just Europe, it is the world.

In the first five years that John was in the firm the retail prices of branded goods, particularly proprietary spirits, were fixed by the manufacturers – Retail Price Maintenance. This prevented cut-pricing and meant traders had to compete on range, quality and service rather than on price. This suddenly came to an end in 1964 when Ted Heath pushed through an Act of Parliament making RPM illegal. There was consternation in the wine and spirit industry. The Chairman of the Hull Brewery Company, a major player in the area through its wine subsidiary, Lambert Parker & Gaines, and its shop subsidiary, Southam's, called a meeting of all the trade. Charles, accompanied by John, attended the meeting. The overwhelming majority of those attending were from brewery-dominated companies. They didn't like John, who was considered 'a young upstart', who had come into an old sleepy company and started rocking the boat by trying to take their business. The aim of the meeting was to get everyone to agree to maintain existing prices. Charles was inclined to agree but John insisted that Townend's would only keep present prices as long as no-one in the city started cutting prices; he chose his words carefully.

A couple of weeks later the local press telephoned John and asked when he was going to cut his prices. He replied, 'Not until somebody else does.' 'They have, already,' the reply came back; S Lambert & Co., a licensed grocer in Whitefriargate, had reduced the price of proprietary gin and whisky. Within 24 hours all Townend's spirit prices were reduced by four shillings a bottle and 24 hours later there was a large advertisement in the *Hull Daily Mail*. The public response was enormous; people were queuing to get into Townend's shops.

Turnover soared and, despite lower margins, profits increased. Of course, eventually the competition responded but it was too late. Townend's kept most of the extra trade and established a reputation for being competitive which lasted at least ten years. John's name was 'mud' in the trade and an action for slander nearly took place because he was accused of having broken his word. The competitors said that he had agreed to keep prices fixed if they did. He didn't. He'd said, 'So long as no-one in the city cuts prices.' From then on it was war.

This was sad for Charles, who did not like confrontation but preferred to be friendly with his competitors. As the end of the century approached, John wryly commented 'that of all the firms represented at that meeting, only the House of Townend remained. They had all sold out or closed down.' In 1964 Charles, aged 65, celebrated 50 years in the wine and spirit trade. The occasion was marked by a celebratory luncheon, organised by John in honour of his father, at the Royal

Station Hotel in Hull. All his local competitors and a number of his friends in the trade, whom he had known for many years, attended.

Eighteen months later there were still pockets around the county where the end of RPM had not affected the Off Licence business. One of these was Scunthorpe. John saw this as a great opportunity; he managed to take a lease in a new development, obtained a licence and opened another self-service wine centre in a large shop. The new branch was launched as a self-service wine centre with a significant advertising campaign, announcing, 'Cut Prices have arrived in Scunthorpe'. Again, it was an immediate success and for a number of years Scunthorpe became the most profitable branch in the Company, so in 1971 the adjoining shop premises were taken in and Home Brew and Greeting Cards departments were added. This was another example of the way John was always looking at ways to develop the business. Unfortunately, in this case it was not successful.

When John joined the firm the average Off Licence was nothing like the wine shop of today. It usually had a limited stock and range of wines, and management knowledge about wine was the exception rather than the rule. John was determined to change this. The shops were enlarged, brightened up and the range of wines increased dramatically. Good quality managers were employed and trained and at the end of John's first ten years the chain of five had become a chain of 21.

As the retail chain increased it became clear that two matters were becoming increasingly urgent:

Buying more competitively to squeeze extra profits out of every sale.
Expanding the infrastructure to service the growing business.

In those days the most economic way to buy wine was to buy in cask, ship it to the UK and bottle on one's own bottling plant. Townend's had bottled spirits and fortified wines since the 1930s but had not imported bulk table wine. John progressively extended imports to include all the major wine areas, except Germany. For example, in 1961 for the first time he shipped over 50 hogs of 1959 Burgundy, including such famous names as Le Corton and Clos Vougeot, and classified Bordeaux included Château Talbot and Château Gruaud-Larose, all of which were bottled in Cave Street. As a result of this the margins on wine increased significantly.

The end of Retail Price Maintenance meant it was essential to buy proprietary goods at better prices to be

Menu card for the luncheon celebrating Charles Townend's fifty years in the trade, 1964.

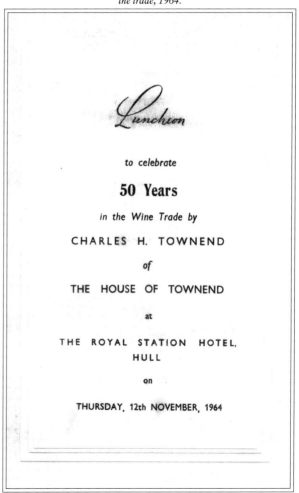

Luncheon

to celebrate

50 Years

in the Wine Trade by

CHARLES H. TOWNEND

of

THE HOUSE OF TOWNEND

at

THE ROYAL STATION HOTEL,
HULL

on

THURSDAY, 12th NOVEMBER, 1964

able to compete with large brewery groups, which were now beginning to dominate the wine and spirits industry. John decided the only way to compete was to buy the same sort of quantities as the Big Boys and the only way that could be feasible was for a number of independent firms to join together and form a

buying group. Following correspondence in *Harpers*, the wine and spirit trade magazine, initiated by a letter from John, in 1965 he called a meeting in York at which 12 wine merchants from various parts of the country formed the IWMA (Independent Wine Merchants Associated), later to become the Merchant Vintners. John was elected Chairman and for 35 years was the driving force until he retired from the post in 2000.

The Company's rapid growth was increasing pressure on the small warehouse in Cave Street. Extra space became an absolute necessity; it was decided that it would be very beneficial if this space could be bonded so payment of duty could be deferred and help the growing requirement for working capital. Raines and Porter's old Varnish Factory in York Street, Wincolmlee, was on the market and it was felt this would be suitable for conversion into a bonded warehouse. Application was made to HM Customs and Excise for permission to open these premises as a Bond, and this was granted, subject to the necessary alterations. This was the first new Bond in Hull for 60 years, and was a real landmark in the Company's

1972 – Scarborough Bond.

1973 – John Townend and Gordon Clare, nose in whiskies during whisky blending session.

history – for the first time the Company could bottle 'Under Bond'. What was really innovative was that the Company managed to persuade Customs to allow them to use the same bottling line for Duty Paid Goods. A new Company, the Hull Bonding Company, was formed to operate the Bond and, due to the rapid expansion of business, in 1966 the Bonding Company became the sole lessee of Scarborough Bond, which had been operated by an old firm in Scarborough, T. Laughton, which was taken over.

After the 1939-45 war, the volume of bottling increased to such an extent that it was not possible to continue bottling by hand. Progressively, semi-automatic machinery was introduced. First was a four-head vacuum filler for bottling and then an 'albro' labeller. Later, an automatic corker was added to the line, but for many years the capsules were still put on by hand. This improved method of bottling was still labour intensive, as each machine needed an operator, but the daily capacity of the line greatly increased. At this time, many bottles were returnable; they were rewashed and reused. In the 1950s, an up-to-date automatic bottle-washing machine was purchased from Thomas Hill, whose factory in Park Lane was adjacent to Cave Street.

Up to the 1960's all bulk wine was imported in casks of various sizes hogsheads, pipes and butts. There was quite a lot of cost involved in importing in cask. First, the cost of the barrels had to be added to the cost of the wine. It was uneconomic to ship the empty cask back and, apart from sherry casks, which were used for filling whisky, second-hand casks in the UK had very little value. Secondly, there was also the risk of damage to casks in transit, and contamination of the wine during shipment. With the move to liquid bulk containerisation, there was some scepticism amongst the traditionalists in the trade. Always at the forefront of change, Townend's had a trial shipment of wine in containers in late 1967. They were the first firm to use this method in the East Riding. The shipment arrived at York Street in early January 1968. The containers were square, of French origin, and called 'Safraps'. They contained the equivalent of 11 hogsheads (3,300 bottles). Constructed of steel, they were lined with a special substance which resisted the corrosion effect of wine, keeping it in perfect condition during the journey. This method of shipping was more economic because the freight and insurance were lower, there was less handling and no cost of casks.

When the containers arrived, the wine had to be pumped straight from the container on the lorry into steel tanks, which were also especially lined, in the York Street Bond. This move to a new system of importation had meant that Townend's had had to install a number of tanks, in which the wine was stored, prior to bottling it in the Bond. Because of the size of containers, only those wines which could be bought in quantities of 11 hogsheads or more could be shipped in this way. These included volume sellers, such as Spanish Table Wine, Yugoslavian Lutomer Riesling, Anjou Rosé and Beaujolais. Other wines continued to be shipped in casks.

The Merchant Vintners imported wine in case and held it in a Central Bond for its members, but it did not have facilities for importing in bulk and bottling. There were four members who had bottling lines – Townend's, Tanner's of Shrewsbury, Moran's of Bristol and Balls Brothers in London, so they bottled Group wines and supplied the other members who were nearest to them. Townend's, for example, supplied all the Merchant Vintner members in the North, Scotland, and the East Midlands. At a later date, Townend's bottled all the Group's vodka, under its Baronoff label. The traditional French Wine Appellations progressively made the bottling of wine, in the area of production, mandatory and they were followed by the Port authorities taking a similar decision, in respect of vintage port. So, Townend's could no longer import Burgundies or Port in bulk.

At the same time, there was a rapid movement into the containerisation of case goods, which were shipped in containers, containing about 1,100 cases. These had great advantages over previous methods and largely eliminated the financial benefits of importing in bulk. One of the great assets was the flexibility: in a container of cased wines you could have as many different wines and styles as you wanted, even as little as 50 cases, whereas a Safrap contained only one wine. As progress continued and Safraps were quite quickly phased out and

replaced for large quantities of bulk wines by road tankers. Bottling only remained advantageous if you could do very large quantities of one line, in which case you could import in these new tankers. The smallest compartment was something like 1,500 gallons, equivalent to between 750 and 800 cases. Townend's were the only firm to use wine road tankers in the Hull area

Traditional method of importing – barrels on a lorry outside the York Street Bond.

Wine imported through the ages

Wine imported in Safrac 550-gallon tanks; wine being checked by John Townend.

Wine imported in road tanker.

and imported the base wine for manufacturing Keeling's. As a result of these changes, Table Wine bottling was rapidly phased out, leaving only the bottling of Port, Sherry, Spirits, Whisky, Gin, Rum, Vodka and Advocaat.

In 1965 John stood as a candidate for Park Ward of Hull City Council. This was the ward his grandfather had sat for and where his offices and cellars were situated. Although in the previous election his party had been bottom of the poll, he only lost by 14 votes. As a reward for doing so well, in 1966 he was asked to fight Newland Ward, once a safe seat, but now held by Councillor Millward, the leader of the Liberals. John knocked her out and quickly made his mark on the Council. Rupert Alec-Smith, the group leader, quickly spotted his abilities, and in 1967 appointed him Opposition Chief Whip and Spokesman on Finance. He became Alderman Leo Schultz's main opponent and their oratorical jousts in finance debates were widely reported in the *Hull Daily Mail*. John was a leader of a group of young councillors who aimed to take control of the City Council, for the first time since the war; he spent a lot of time encouraging people to stand. When they took control in 1969, they had a fantastic line-up – a barrister, who became a judge; two of the city's leading solicitors; two accountants; an architect; an estate agent; the deputy head of Endsleigh College; the President of the Junior Chamber of Shipping and Commerce; businessmen from Horsley Smith, Fenners, Needler's, Slingsby's and Hammonds; a wine merchant, a pet food retailer; a property man and two directors of horticultural companies. They all gave their time, knowledge and experience, without payment; today, most people of that calibre would not be seen dead on a council and those that are prepared to serve are paid many thousands of pounds.

John still remembers the pleasure on election night of winning control after many years of defeats, and the Guildhall resounding to the sound of *Land of Hope and Glory,* as opposed to the usual *Red Flag.* John was immediately appointed Chairman of the Finance Committee and the Reorganisation Committee. As such, be brought in McKinseys, the International Management Consultants, to identify inefficiencies in the way the Council operated. It was not very difficult.

This, however, was a revolutionary action for a city council to take. John became Chairman of the Humber Bridge Board and was responsible for the successful negotiations with the Minister that enabled the Board to borrow the funds needed to build the bridge. Considering what happened after he ceased to be Chairman, when the costs soared, it might have been better if he had not succeeded!

As a result of his efforts on the Council, he was considered an ideal candidate to fight the North Hull Constituency in the 1970 General Election, but, as expected, he was defeated. When the Hull Council was abolished, John was elected to Humberside County Council and became Leader of the Opposition. Four years later he led his party to victory at the election and became the Leader of the Council. Having included it in the manifesto, his first action was to abolish the 'closed shop'. This was another groundbreaking action for a local authority.

All this activity took John away from his business. Because so many of his group, like him, were successful busy people with limited time, John, both as a Chairman and a Leader, tried to ensure that unnecessary meetings were not called and that meetings were conducted expeditiously. He used to say, 'It's not our job to run the local authority; we appoint the people who run it, we monitor them and if need be, sack them. We fix the policy and they implement it.' To make up for business time that he lost whilst in the Council, he would start early, work for a couple of hours, jump into his car and five minutes later he would be in the Council office in the centre of Hull, ensure the meeting didn't last more than a couple of hours and be back in his office to work over lunchtime. He always had a briefcase full of papers to work on at home.

The 1960s started with the dead hand of the family being lifted; this, coupled with an enthusiastic, dynamic young man in the top management, meant that it was a decade of real success, particularly on the retail side of the business. At the end of the decade John was appointed to the Board of Gale Lister; that had many implications for the future of the Company, but that story has a chapter to itself.

Chapter 8:

The Gale Lister Episode 1968

This episode was to result in enormous opportunities for the Company, which eventually turned into disaster, almost destroying the firm.

As a result of his friendship with Louis Porter, Charles had had a small shareholding in Gale Lister, a company in Leeds, ever since it became a public company. John, who was always interested in stocks and shares, kept an eye on the share price. One day in 1966 John noticed the share price had suddenly collapsed. He felt either the company was going broke or it was a marvellous buying opportunity. He rang Tom Porter, Louis's son and the then Managing Director, to see what he could find out. Tom told him they were not going broke; he had no idea why the share price had collapsed. John immediately rang his stockbroker and bought a parcel of shares, as did his mother and father.

Gale Lister had not done well since Louis Porter's death. His son Tom had gone virtually straight from Sedbergh into the Army during the war and then into the firm, without having any training or experience. John felt some new blood was required so he wrote to the Chairman, William Tweedle, the senior partner in the well-known Leeds solicitors, Simpson Curtis, and suggested he should be invited to join the Board. After a meeting with Mr. Tweedle, this offer was rejected.

In early 1968 the shareholders of Gale Lister received notification that the directors had agreed to a merger between the company and Joseph Hobson Ltd and its associate, Thomas Walker & Co. (York) Limited. These two companies were private companies and the deal was, in fact, a reverse takeover, which put Hobson's Managing Director, Kenneth Pawson, in the driving seat. The terms were very much weighted against Gale Lister's shareholders as they were going to see a significant part of their equity converted to preference shares. Hobson's were to receive redeemable loan notes for their property and more than half of the ordinary shares of the merged company.

John thought this was a poor deal and discussed it with his close friend, Barry Appleyard, who was also a small shareholder in Gale Lister. John suggested it would be 'interesting' to oppose the deal and he asked Barry if he would join with him in sending out a circular to all shareholders, urging them to turn down the proposals. Barry agreed and so they obtained from the Companies Registrar a list of the names and addresses of the company's shareholders. They then drafted a circular, which pointed out that Gale Lister's shareholders would contribute £233,754 of net assets compared with Hobson's £184,427, but would have only 29% of the equity and a holding worth only £160,000 compared with Hobson's £240,000. They both signed the circular, which was reproduced on Townend's office duplicator and duly circulated. When they had received the list of shareholders they had been amazed to see the large number of small shareholders, many of whom were customers or former customers. There were very few large shareholders and if you took the holdings of John, his mother and father together, they were the second largest. The directors responded to the circular by sending a counter-communication dated 22 March 1968. A battle for proxies developed and John and Barry started ringing all the medium-sized shareholders. The directors retaliated and so the battle continued into the eve of the Extraordinary General Meeting, which was called for Monday, 1 April, at which the merger was to be approved.

The day came and the offices in The Calls were packed with shareholders. The Chairman led the directors in and opened the meeting by explaining the rationale behind the merger proposal. John made an impassioned speech (shades of things to come) urging shareholders not to sell the majority of the equity on the cheap. The vote was then taken, the resolution was passed but John and Barry demanded a poll and, when the votes and proxies were counted, the resolution did not have the required 75% majority, so the directors' proposals failed.

You can imagine the consternation this caused. Mr. Tweedle closed the meeting, asking Mr. Townend, Mr. Appleyard and their financial advisers to stay behind and meet the directors. When everyone had gone there was only John and Barry left, Mr. Tweddle asked, 'Where are your advisers?' John replied, 'We don't have any.' He looked surprised, 'But who did your circulars?' John replied, 'We did and printed them on our office duplicator'.

He said, 'You have put us in some difficulty. Would you consider doing a similar deal to the one we had with Hobson's? You sell J. Townend & Sons to Gale Lister's for shares and you will then be in the driving seat.'

Clearly what Mr. Tweddle wanted to do was to get rid of a troublesome and possible embarrassing chairmanship as quickly as possible. John said, 'I would have to consider the matter.' When he got home to Hull he thought long and hard. On the one hand, it could be a great opportunity. Townend's would become a public company, which the family would control. This could be a vehicle to get into the big time. On the other hand, there were disadvantages. With a Plc, you cannot treat the company as if it is yours. There could be no automatic right for his children to take over, even if they had the ability.

Because the management was poor, John would have to go and live in Leeds and take over the day-to-day management. All his friends were in East Yorkshire, he was beginning to build up a political career, being one of the leading Tories on Hull Council and he had just been adopted as the Parliamentary candidate to fight the North Hull constituency. He decided to turn the opportunity down so he withdrew his opposition to the deal, provided Hobson's improved the terms by increasing the coupon on the preference shares from 6.5% to 7%, increase the number of shares going to the Gale Lister shareholders from 35,000 to 40,000 and reduce the amount of loan stock going to Hobson's by £5,000. In addition, John was to be made a director of the merged company.

The Boards of the two companies quickly agreed to these proposals and the deal went through and John became a director of a public company. In his enthusiasm he omitted to negotiate a fee. He never received any remuneration for the whole time of his directorship. Tweddle resigned as Chairman and the new Chairman,

S. Whatling, was a close friend of Ken Pawson's, who was the new power. After the merger there were clearly too many chiefs and, when the chips were down, it was Tom Porter who went, leaving Ken Pawson in the seat of power.

In the 1930s the Company had developed a large trade in manufacturing cocktails such as Green Goddess, Late Night Final, Damson Cream and Egg Flip. After the war fashions changed and the sales of these drinks progressively declined. The business needed rationalisation and the Board decided to come out of manufacturing except for Bronte Liqueur. John, always with an eye to an opportunity, thought that, if he could add on this manufacturing business to Townend's with little increase in costs, it would be a great investment. A deal was negotiated and it was agreed that Townend's would take over these brands. The manufacturing equipment was taken over at book value, the raw material stocks at cost. There was to be no payment for goodwill but Townend's did agree to take over some worthless advertising material, show cards etc. at book value.

A problem arose because Gale Lister was a public company, John was a director and the assets being transferred were considered significant. The deal would have to be approved at a shareholders' meeting. To avoid this inconvenience, instead of the ownership of the brands becoming Townend's property, they took a long-term licence on a payment of a nominal annual payment per case sold. In 1971 the production was finally moved to Hull and the tanks and manufacturing equipment were installed at Red Duster House. The first attempt to make Egg Flip was a disaster and the liquid separated.

This showed there was more to it than just having the recipe! John compared it to housewives baking a cake from the same recipe but with one producing a much better cake than the other. The problem was overcome by employing Gale Lister's retired Production Director, Arnold Forest, as a consultant. He came and supervised the next mixture, trained Ian Stamper, Townend's Works' Director, and from then on all was well.

At about the time the agreement with Gale Lister was signed, Jim Moggridge was recommended to the Company by Brian Oughtred of William Jackson. Jim was coming to the area in order to marry Vicky Hibbert, a local girl, and he had approached Jackson's through her father, Ken, who was involved with Jackson's. Because at this stage the wine and spirits' sales at Jacksons were relatively small they did not have room for such a highly qualified executive. John interviewed him and decided that with the growth of the business he needed someone to take over responsibility for sales. The takeover of the Gale Lister brand made the timing especially appropriate.

John was aware the brands he had taken over were slowly dying. However, they were high margin lines and were absorbed in existing overheads, adding a useful throughput to the bottling line. This gave a welcome boost in short-term profitability, but, more importantly, gave the Company expertise in manufacturing egg-based drinks. This led to Keeling's Advocaat, which is a story in itself.

Green Goddesses operated by the Royal Air Force to keep services going during a strike, receiving a case of Green Goddess for their crew.

Chapter 9:

The Defeat of the Unions

John had become very opposed to the Unions because of the damage they were doing to the country generally and particularly to the way the TWGU on the Hull Docks was ruining the commerce of the city of his birth. By abusing their power under the National Dock Labour Scheme, the TGWU had bought the port of Hull to its knees to such an extent that the City had dropped from its position as the third largest port in the UK, after London and Liverpool, to the twentieth; whereas Felixstowe, which was not a NDLB Scheme Port and was not Union dominated, had risen from the bottom of the league to the top.

John was also opposed in principle to Unions being in family businesses because he felt they destroyed the team spirit and created a 'them and us' situation. A good example of what damage Unions can do to private firms was the case of Weeks Trailers, a non-Union company, founded by two West Indian/English brothers, which had been very successful. The elder brother had been a close friend of John's. After they floated the company, the Unions managed to get established and, due to militant shop stewards, it eventually shut down and the workers all ended up on the dole.

When one morning in the early 70s he opened the post he came across a letter from the Transport and General Workers' Union. An immediate feeling of apprehension came over him. When he read the letter apprehension turned to alarm verging on panic. The letter was from the local union secretary and said they had recruited over half the members of the company (the figure turned out to be an exaggeration) and he would like to arrange a meeting to discuss a recognition agreement. As a leading Opposition councillor on Hull City Council, John had bravely spoken out about the damaging effect Union power was having on the city. He was convinced his Company had been targeted because of his criticisms of the Unions and his political views. He felt he would not be able to continue in a Union environment and he would sell the business.

A similar situation had arisen some time previously at the Shrewsbury firm of Tanner's, which was a member of the Merchant Vintners. Richard Tanner, with the help of a consultant, had fought a long battle to keep them out. In the end he had won but only after having shut down his Shrewsbury beer distribution warehouse, where most of the Union members were employed. John immediately rang Richard for his advice and obtained an introduction to Robert Freeman, the consultant Tanner's had used. He then spoke to Robert on the telephone, who told him to do nothing until they had a meeting. 'It is vital,' he said, 'that no one knows you are taking advice, especially from me, because I have a reputation with Unions. Therefore, we must meet outside Hull.' A meeting was quickly set up in a hotel somewhere in the Nottinghamshire area.

At the meeting Robert said, 'The first question I must ask you is do you wish to get the Unions out, or do you wish me to negotiate the best deal I can for you?' 'Get them out,' said John. 'Right,' Robert replied. 'Your only chance is to get them out now. We must plan this like a military campaign.'. 'First, intelligence. We need to know what they are doing, who their leaders are, who has joined and, most importantly, who is the collector of the subscriptions. At the same time we must deny them intelligence of what we are doing. Therefore, you will not ring me through the switchboard and when I ring you I will just say this is your friend Robert calling. You need, if possible, to have an informant from the shop floor, probably a loyal, long serving-employee who hasn't joined and is supportive of the family. In order to encourage recruitment the Union will have made lots of promises to your staff about increases in wages. The new members will be paying their weekly Union dues and will expect a quick return. If we stretch it out for months some will get tired of paying their subscriptions and drop out. Thirdly, you mustn't meet the Unions or speak to them on the phone if at all possible. Ignore the first letter and in due course you will get a reminder and we will discuss what to do then.'

When John got back to his office he set up a 'Council of War' with Gordon Clare, the General Manager, and Ian Stamper, the Warehouse and Production Manager.

They decided to talk to one of their most senior employees, Walter Redhead, who drove one of the vans. He had been with the firm many years and was considered to be an old family retainer. John invited him into the office and asked him what he knew about the Unions. 'I am against them,' he said. 'I have told them I want nothing to do with them.' It turned out that he was prepared to be very helpful and wanted to see the company get them out. He identified the leader and subscription collector, who was a van driver, whom we will call 'J', who had only been with the firm eight months. John was not surprised as he had noticed the man a couple of weeks after he had started working for the firm and when he spoke to him he found that he was very surly and did not seem to have the attitude that was encouraged in a family firm. John had spoken to Ian Stamper, who said he was very good and efficient. John said, 'Keep an eye on him and if he steps out of line, let me know.' Cleverly he never put a foot wrong for six months. The week after the completion of the six months he was under the protection of the employment legislation and could bring an Unfair Dismissal case against the company. The following week he brought out the Union application forms and started recruiting. Walter also identified two other keen supporters.

Walter told John that the others who had joined were apathetic and had only gone along with the Union in the hope of a speedy increase in wages. No one in the office or shops had joined. Walter said he would collect intelligence and report back regularly. Armed with this information, a further meeting with Robert was set up. He suggested the Company needed, if possible, to get rid of the collector and his two main supporters. After a lot of discussion a plan was agreed. The Company was always very busy prior to Christmas, but trade is normally very low in January and February, and, this particular year, trade in January was even worse than normal, so the Company was overmanned. It was decided to take one van off the road, so one van driver would have to be made redundant. John consulted Robert as to how this unfortunate person should be selected. Robert said, 'In view of your problems, you must go by the book – last in, first out.' So, fortunately,

'J' was made redundant. A postscript to this was that the redundant driver, whom John was convinced was a Union plant, took the Company to an Industrial Court, but, because he had got another job immediately after he left, the damages awarded against the Company were minimal.

While this was all taking place a reminder from the Union asking for a reply to the previous letter was received. Fortunately, it was addressed to the Company Secretary. After a suitable delay the Secretary acknowledged the letter and said he had referred it to the directors. In due course another letter arrived and the Company Secretary replied to say it was on the agenda for the next Board meeting. What he did not say was that this was an owner-managed company and only had one Board meeting a year!

After the Union plant left, the collecting of Union subs was taken over by one of the ladies on the bottling line. By this time the bottling staff, warehousemen and drivers were split into two camps – non-Union and the Union. They even had separate tea breaks. The battle for Union recognition continued. Union dues were being paid each week and still no wage increase had been achieved. All the Union members were worse off. They began to become very dissatisfied. The TGWU called a meeting at their headquarters, Bevin House. The intelligence man told Townend's the time, date and place and Gordon Clare, the General Manager, dressed himself up in an old mac, cap and muffler, borrowed an old car and parked himself within sight of the entrance of Bevin House. He then made a list of all the staff who attended.

The Company found out the Union organiser had told them 'they would never get the better of that "bastard" Townend, unless they went on strike'. This suggestion did not go down well and one person said, 'We did not join the Union to go on strike. We joined the Union for more money.' The upshot was the next day at the tea break they decided to leave the TGWU and all tore up their Union cards. The irony is that when the members tore up their cards, they thought they were rid of the TGWU. But there was no mechanism for resigning from Trade Unions, and, when the TGWU celebrated achieving two million members shortly afterwards, those misguided Townend employees, like thousands of others across the country, were in the total.

The battle was over. Game, set and match to the Company and to those who had stayed loyal. Townend's had been saved by the enlightened self-interest of the workers responding to the family's leadership. If other parts of British industry had been lucky enough to have such leaders and employees in those days, much lost pain and suffering would have been avoided by UK Limited. Given the present legislation, it is unlikely the Company could have achieved the same result now. If the Unions had won, John said he would have sold up to another multiple, who would have closed the warehouse and offices and just kept the shops. There would be no House of Townend and no centenary. There was one lesson that was learnt from this episode, and that was the vital need to have good, regular communication between the shop floor and the management.

John had another victory over the Unions. He had always been opposed to the principle of the 'closed shop', as he felt it infringed the freedom of the individual worker.

The Opposition on Humberside County Council under John's leadership included in their 1977 election manifesto that if they gained control they would abolish any closed shops operating in council departments. They won the election and John tore up the closed shop agreements, as he had been given a mandate by the electorate. Surprisingly, all threats of industrial action came to nothing. Ten years later, the government made closed shops illegal. Just another example of John being ahead of the game.

Chapter 10:

The 1970s

At the beginning of the decade it became clear that the Cave Street premises were becoming too small for the volume of trade. Furthermore, the premises were not suitable for modern handling methods such as palletisation and fork lift trucks. Having the despatch department and the administration on one site and the bottling and the Bond on another, was expensive and inefficient. It was decided to concentrate the Company's operation on the York Street site and dispose of the original Cave Street premises. Plans were drawn up and a contract placed to erect a new Duty Paid warehouse and office block adjoining the Bond. A small trade Cash and Carry was incorporated in the scheme to supply the licensed trade, corporate customers, and large private buyers. The bottling hall was doubled in size and additional vats were installed so the Company could progressively move to importing wine in 550-gallon containers instead of wooden hogsheads and barrels.

John wanted to celebrate this quantum leap forward with a grand opening. Charles, never one for the limelight and self-publicity, was reluctant to agree. John eventually convinced him around but Charles made one stipulation. 'If the Company was going to do it, it had to be done well with no expense spared.' John, who was always trying to cut costs, freely admits that on this occasion his father was right with this philosophy – if you can't do it well, don't do it at all.

Then the question was who should perform the official opening? This resulted in a major discussion. Somebody came up with, 'Let's invite the most influential man in the European wine industry.' The first name that came to mind was Comte Robert-Jean de Vogüé, the head of Moët Hennessy. Robert was an outstanding personality who had a remarkable life. During the war he was very involved with the Resistance and had been condemned to death by the Nazis. He became very well known in the UK as a result of being the subject of one of Alan

Whicker's famous programmes, 'Great Men of Europe'. He was clearly the ideal choice, but would he come? Patrick Forbes, the Managing Director of Moët, London, was approached and asked if he thought the Count would come; Townend's said they could be flexible with the date. To their delight the invitation was accepted and the date fixed for 5 June 1972.

The guest list was drawn up and included the Lord Mayor of Hull, the Town Clerk, the Sheriff, the French Vice Consul, the Vice-Chancellor of the University and leading business and professional men of the area, together with suppliers from abroad and even local competitors. The premises, both the old and the new, had to be immaculate. The organisation was run like a military operation. One warehouse was completely emptied, lined with drapes and laid out with tables for lunch, which was to be provided by Derek Baugh, the Managing Director of the newly formed Townend Catering Company, based at the Nag's Head, Routh.

The great day arrived and the gods looked kindly on; it was a beautiful sunny day. Charles departed from Red Duster House in a chauffeur-driven Rolls Royce to meet the Count at Brough aerodrome. The Count's Champagne-coloured jet swept out of the sky and made a perfect landing. He was accompanied by his daughter-in-law, Comtesse Catherine de Vogüé, who had stood in at the last moment for her mother-in-law, who had suddenly been taken ill. The Count brought with him

1971 – Topping out ceremony of the new York Street offices and Duty Paid stores.

Napoleon's hat, which his company had recently purchased. It was the first time it had been in England and after the opening he was taking it to Castle Howard to put it in an exhibition.

John had been left at the ranch to oversee the final organisation. A marquee had been erected adjoining the garage for the reception and opening ceremony. The Count was introduced by Charles and he then said a few words, declared the building, now named Red Duster House, open and unveiled a commemorative plaque in the reception. The guests were then divided into groups and given a guided tour of all the premises. When the official party had completed the tour they returned to the Boardroom where Count Robert signed two commemorative plates especially produced for the occasion; one remained at Townend's and one was for him.

A Champagne reception, Moët & Chandon, of course, was followed by a celebration lunch. It was hard to imagine one was in a wine warehouse for the walls had been lined with drapes and the tables set with sparkling white tablecloths, glass and cutlery. The magnificent lunch was naturally accompanied by magnificent wines. After the meal there were three speeches; Charles, the Chairman, welcomed the Count and other guests in a very witty speech and spoke of the past and the inevitable problems that family business face. In reply, the Count made a magnificent speech in excellent English (no one

1972 – Opening of the new stores by Comte Robert-Jean de Vogüé, who opened the new York Street premises and brought with him Napoleon's hat. Left to right: John Townend; Comte Robert-Jean de Vogüé; his daughter-in-law, Comtesse Catherine de Vogüé, and Charles Townend.

present could have done the same in French) and proposed a toast to the Company, to which John responded, speaking of his hopes for the future. At the end of the proceedings Charles presented the Count, who was a collector of antique silver, with a George III Loving Cup, as a memento of his visit. The Company produced a hardback commemorative booklet for the occasion, which gave a brief resumé about the Company's history and the involvement of the Townend family. Each guest was presented with a copy.

After the guests had all gone and the Count had departed for Castle Howard, John and Charles and their wives gathered in the Boardroom and were amazed that all the planning had paid off and there had been no snags. It had been a memorable day, which had lifted the perception of the Company both locally and nationally. It was a milestone in the Company's history. The star had, of course, been the Count and people still talk of his visit 30 years later.

In 1973 the company took a major step in appointing non-family directors to the Board for the first time. Gordon Clare, the General Manager, and Jim Moggridge, the Sales Manager, were both appointed to the Board.

This decade was dominated by Keeling's Old English Advocaat but there were also other important developments. On the retail front, a wine shop in Stonegate Road, Leeds, was purchased in 1970. The property was leased but John managed to obtain an option to purchase at a fixed price. Shortly afterwards property prices soared and, when the shop became uneconomic in the early 1980s, John bought the premises at the 1970 price, closed the shop and made a substantial profit on the sale of the property.

In 1974 a large licensed grocer's, A. G. Dosser, situated in the Market Place at Hedon, was purchased. The small House of Townend branch, opposite, was closed and the business transferred to the new premises. The larger premises were completely refurbished and John's wife, Jennifer, did the designs on traditional lines. When the shop reopened the groceries had been eliminated and it had become a very attractive specialist wine shop. Over the next few years Hedon became one of the Company's best branches. Licences were also acquired in Gypsyville,

Hull (1975), Bransholme Centre (1976) and Southcoates Lane, Hull (1979). In 1978 an Off Licence in Orchard Park, Hull, was purchased from Mr. G. Holmes.

The Withernsea branch was moved to new premises in the main shopping street, and adjacent premises used as a Highways Depot were acquired at Ferriby and the whole site redeveloped. Selling groceries was not very interesting, so the Yeadon branch was leased to the manager. Davenport's, a high-class licensed grocery in Filey, was purchased in 1979 but in this case it was decided to continue groceries.

In 1973 the Company bought a business in Elland, which traded under the name of Thomas Bros. It was a general wholesaler of beer and wines and spirits including draught beers. Geoff Potts, the son-in-law of the former owner, stayed with the Townend's and became the manager. Going back into the wholesale beer business was a departure from John's overall strategy and was, in a way, going back to the family's origins in the liquor business. The premises fronted onto the main street and the front was quickly turned into a retail shop, which traded under the House of Townend banner. Shortly after the purchase of these premises, the bank at the corner was closed and the bank put up for sale the bank premises and three adjoining Let shops; these were bought at a knockdown price. In some parts of the country wine bars were beginning to open up and became popular. Therefore, it was decided to take the opportunity of converting the bank premises into a new wine bar. This was made quite attractive and was put under the supervision of Derek Baugh, the Managing Director of the Willerby Manor Hotel. Unfortunately, the Company was a bit ahead of the times and what might be popular around London was not, as yet, so popular in the very traditional West Riding of Yorkshire.

Chapter 11:

Keeling's Advocaat

As a result of the takeover of Gale Lister's drinks manufacturing operation the Company acquired the technical know-how of manufacturing egg-based drinks and wine-based drinks. John became interested in manufacturing Advocaat, which, like Eggflip, was an egg-based alcoholic drink. He found there was no set recipe and no geographical connotation; Advocaat was made mainly in Holland but also in Germany, Belgium and the Channel Isles. The Dutch advertised incorrectly that it was made from brandy, the distillation of the grape, when in fact it was made from the base spirit of Dutch gin, which had never seen a grape. In the Channel Islands it included cream, while in Belgium it was already made from a wine base.

As Advocaat from Holland, which included the brand leader, was made from a spirit base, it paid the spirit duty. John came up with the idea that if Townend's could make an Advocaat of good quality from a wine fortified with brandy, it would pay the much lower fortified wine duty and have a competitive advantage. The problem was to get the base wine as neutral as possible to make the taste similar to the Dutch Advocaat. The strength was the same because water was added to spirit-based Advocaat to reduce the strength. To achieve the right strength it was necessary to bring wine with as high a strength as allowed and pay the fortified wine duty. It also had to be as neutral as possible to get the right taste.

John sourced the wine known as Water White from a Cypriot winery in Limmasol. Once the product was perfected, a decision had to be made as to the name, the packaging and the marketing; he didn't like the sound of 'Townend's Advocaat'. Because Townend's were large retailers and wanted to sell to the trade it was thought it would be better to keep Townend's name out of it. John sat down with the Sales Director, Jim Moggridge, to see if they could come up with a suitable name. Someone suggested the name Keeling's. This was the name of a family partnership, which owned several retails shops in the West Riding; this name was agreed – a decision that was to have far-reaching effects, as H. Keeling & Co., being a partnership, made all the partners liable for all the costs and damages in the event of any action being taken against the Company.

John then dreamed up the slogan, 'You get wonderful feelings when you drink Keeling's'. All that was left now was to print the labels, make the product and launch the brand, which the Company did in July 1974. The difference between the spirit duty and the wine duty was so great that the Company could undercut the brand leaders by a significant amount, leaving a large margin and sufficient to have a generous advertising budget. Jim, as the Sales Manager, was put in charge of sales but John got the first large account when he was invited to lunch with Comte Robert-Jean de Vogüé at Moët & Chandon's office in London. There was only one other guest, Ray Gough, trading as Gough Brothers in the London area. John told him about his new product and how competitive it was and Ray agreed to take Keeling's for all his shops. In the period to December 1974, only five months, 5,000 cases were sold. Jim took on a dedicated sales representative and then, as trade built up, more, until the sales team consisted of him and four salesmen. The grocery trade, particularly Cash and Carry's and supermarkets, were a large market and 80% of the production was sold in the run up to Christmas.

At Christmas 1975 the brand was advertised on Trident and Granada TV for the first time and sold about 20,000 cases. In 1976 it was advertised in seven TV areas at a cost of £108k and sold almost 60,000 cases. Due to the court cases, advertising on TV was suspended and sales in 1977 dropped to 35,000. By judgement day in 1979 1.34 million bottles or 152,839 cases had been sold. The Company supplied most of the major food companies – Asda, International Stores, Co-op, Allied Suppliers, William Morrison, Hillards, large Cash and Carry's such as Bookers and multiple chains of wine shops such as Augustus Barnett and Gough Bros. The only two exceptions were Tesco and Sainsbury's and they were poised to take the brand as soon as the case was won in the House of Lords. As part of the marketing programme a 1 ½ mile race, the Keeling's Old English Advocaat

Stakes at Beverley Race Course, was sponsored on 30 April 1977. It was a beautiful day; major customers were invited to lunch in a marquee. The race was televised and the trophy presented by John Townend cost £150; the prize money was £2,100.

The rapid increase in the sale of Keeling's put enormous pressure on manufacturing and storage capacity. Bottling almost 750,000 bottles a year was going to be difficult but the fact that 80% of sales were in November/December created major logistical problems. The Company had to be able to receive bulk road tankers of the base wine and store the wine until used in the manufacturing process. Large tanks were installed in the warehouse adjoining the Bond, along the whole length, two high, on both sides. Large mixing tanks were installed in the Bond. The bottling line was modernised and the semi-automatic machines replaced by automatic ones. Townend's could receive the raw material and produce the Advocaat, but, because they had to build up stocks from the end of August, they had to be able to have space for large quantities of new bottles and tens of thousands of cases of Advocaat, ready for sale.

1977 – John Townend presenting the prize to the owner of the winning horse of the Keeling's Advocaat Stakes, Beverley.

The existing premises could not cope so in 1976 the Company acquired Swift's Lion Copperworks, a large warehouse on the opposite side of Wincolmlee. This was turned into an additional Bond and could hold approximately 40,000 cases. The only disadvantage was that forklift trucks had to move empty bottles and full cases across the road, which got busier by the year. This was quite dangerous and caused much worry, so when in 1979 the Company was able to buy the adjoining premises, which ran from York Street through to Oxford Street, from the Humber Pickle Company they were able to transfer all the stock from the old Copperworks into the newly acquired warehouse that had been converted into a Bond. They put the surplus premises up for sale. The new property also provided warehouse and office space and the opportunity for a much larger Cash & Carry with its own car park.

John always believed, if at all possible, one should buy the adjoining property, if it came up for sale, for future expansion; so when in the same year the property on the other side, a derelict old chapel adjoining the car park, came on the market, this too was acquired.

1976 – Containers of base wine for the manufacture of Keeling's Advocaat, flown in to meet rapidly rising sales.

Chapter 12:

The Keeling's Case

Shortly after the brand was launched a letter was received from Allied Breweries, the parent Company of Warninks Advocaat, objecting to the use of the words 'Keeling's Advocaat' on the grounds that there had been a court case that decided that the word 'Advocaat' on its own indicated that the product was Dutch. Not wishing to have any trouble, the Company agreed to reprint the labels using the words 'Old English Advocaat'. On 17 October 1974, Allied objected to the neck label, which had just the word 'Advocaat', so this was changed to accommodate them.

In the meantime, on 29 August 1974 a letter was received from HM Customs & Excise stating that 'Keeling's Old English Advocaat, prepared from imported wines contravenes Section 152 of the Customs & Excise Act 1952 in that the use of the word Advocaat indicated that this is, or is a substitute for, a description of spirits and no further supplies should be supplied for sale'. The Company solicitor, Leslie Davies of Iveson's, was consulted and he wrote back on 30 August challenging the Customs' interpretation of the meaning of the word Advocaat.

Nothing was heard for six months and then on 28 February 1975 another letter was received. Finally on 17 April the Company was informed they were to be taken to Court. As this would be a Treasury case it would be classed as a Criminal Action. On 4 April Allied Breweries wrote, stating that they were going to take a Civil Action, accusing Townend's of 'Passing Off'. They served a writ on 4 August 1975 but their lawyers agreed not to proceed until the Customs' Case had been decided.

In the Customs' Case Townend's were summoned to appear on 22 August 1975 before the Stipendiary Magistrate at the Guildhall, Hull. There were more delays and the case was finally heard on 21 October 1975. Townend's were represented by James Comyn QC. He was a brilliant Irish advocate and tore the Customs' case to shreds to such an extent that when the prosecution finished its case he

persuaded the judge to dismiss the case on the basis that the prosecution had failed to make out a case to answer. The Company was awarded all its costs.

The Customs decided to Appeal and the Appeal was heard at the Crown Court on 20-22 January 1976 before Judge Walker. Comyn again represented Townend's and Mr. Finley, the Customs & Excise. In his summing up the Judge said 'that Townend's had acted with complete propriety at all stages'. The heart of the case was 'Did the word 'Advocaat' indicate that the liqueur was a description of spirits? The Judge found in favour of Townend's and in his judgement said, 'Advocaat is an alcoholic egg drink and not more than that.' He also tellingly said, 'If I had been deciding this on the basis of a Civil Action, I think it is likely I would have decided it in favour of the Respondents [i.e. Townend's].' Costs were again awarded to the Company.

The Company now faced a Civil Action brought by Victoria Wine and Warninks Advocaat, both subsidiaries of Allied Breweries. James Comyn originally said, 'the Criminal case would be 50/50 but you would walk away with a Civil Action', so Townend's entered the case with some confidence. A lot of work had to be done getting respected people in the trade, wine merchants, wine writers and chemists to give evidence on behalf of the defence. The case commenced in July in the High Court, Chancery Division; it was scheduled to take one week. Townend's were represented by James Comyn QC, Allied Brewery by not less than two QC's and Juniors. Clearly they were piling up the costs and they drew out the case to three weeks with a consequent escalation of costs.

There was an ominous sign that the Judge had made up his mind when on the first day he picked up a bottle of Warninks and said, 'Is this the genuine one?' The case seemed to go well and Townend's were able to produce evidence that the Dutch had made Advocaat from a wine base before the war and that the Belgians were still making a wine-based Advocaat. They were very confident they would win. Everyone was devastated when the Judge found against the firm and said the evidence about the Belgium Advocaat was not relevant because it had never been sold in England. The Judge awarded Allied all their costs and damages.

An Appeal was lodged, together with a request that, while awaiting the decision, Keeling's could continue being sold. This was granted. It was six months before the Appeal and, just before the due date at Court, James Comyn was made a Judge and so Townend's had to get another QC. They were represented by Mr. John C. Griffiths, who clearly did a good job because the three judges in the Court of Appeal unanimously ruled in Townend's favour and awarded costs to the defendant. The Company thought they were home and dry and could see their brand becoming number one in the UK market. Warninks and Allied, however, applied for Leave to Appeal to the House of Lords, and this was granted.

One of John's friends said, 'Poor you. At the moment the House of Lords and the Court of Appeal are at loggerheads and, if the Court of Appeal find in your favour, you've a good chance of losing in the House of Lords.' He certainly was proved right. The Company had another serious blow before the case came up as their QC, who had won in the Court of Appeal, was appointed to the post of Attorney General of Hong Kong and sailed from England a short time before the case commenced. Townend's had to get another barrister at the last minute. I don't know if it was his fault but Leslie Davies, Townend's solicitor, told John after the first day of the Appeal that their case had collapsed and they would lose. He was proved right – they were awarded costs and damages. The decision in May 1979 came at a terrible time for John, personally and the Company, as he had just been elected to Parliament. This meant at the very time the Company had received a devastating blow to its profitability and put its very survival at risk at a time when the driving force was missing for most of the week in Westminster.

The case had been going on for almost five years and there was a certain relief that it was all over. But it wasn't; Allied put in a ridiculous claim for almost £3.5 million of damages. They claimed that all of their drop in sales was due to Keeling's Advocaat, ignoring the fact that the launch and rise of Bailey's Cream had hit the whole of the Advocaat market. Naturally, Townend's challenged these assumptions and after a year had made no progress with them. The Company's solicitors informed Townend's that if agreement could not be reached it would have to be settled by the Court and, with the Right of Appeal, they could be faced with another two or three years of litigation, with all the ensuing Costs. Because the defendants had not only been J. Townend & Sons (Hull) Limited but also H. Keeling & Co., a family partnership, the Townend's were all personally liable. At that stage the total family wealth, including the business was between £2-2.5 million, so in a worst stage scenario the whole family could be bankrupt.

If it had been today, the firm would probably have appealed to the European Court and, because of the Belgian Advocaat, they would probably have won, but by the end of the case they were 'punch drunk' and never thought of the European Court, which 25 years ago was still in its infancy. They'd spent three years haggling over the damages and it had had a debilitating effect on the company, which had great difficulty in recruiting good executives. No one wanted to join a company that was facing bankruptcy. This was a particular problem when Gordon Clare, who had taken over as MD when John went into Parliament, retired early. In the end, John took over the position of MD again, although he was in Westminster for most of the week. No major expansions could be undertaken and to build up cash the Nag's Head was sold.

By 1982 John felt he would be retiring before the litigation ended so he decided to bypass the Managing Director of Victoria Wine and approach Keith Showering, the Chairman of the holding company, Allied Breweries. In his letter, John posed the question, 'Was it really in their interest to destroy the business and bankrupt all the members of the family, including his wife and Charles Townend's widow?' He pointed out that as a bankrupt he would have to resign his seat in Parliament and would be entitled to make a personal statement to the House, in which he would explain the reasons in full and illustrate how a big national company was deliberately destroying a family and a family business. John received a rather curt reply in which Showering said that 'Townend's had not shown any regrets or remorse' (of course they hadn't, because they thought they'd done nothing wrong). However,

Showering said he had instructed his people to settle the case.

As a result, the negotiations sprang to life. The figure of £3.5 million was swiftly abandoned and the new brief was to extract the maximum possible without making the family bankrupt and the Company going into liquidation. John recalls having to go to a meeting with his solicitor to meet the MD of Victoria Wines, who had been 'the nigger in the wood pile', at their solicitor's office in London. The man was very arrogant and wanted to know if he had any land or any surplus cash. John replied, 'Educating four children at private school doesn't leave you any surplus cash.' After a lot of haggling, in the end it cost the Company around £0.5 million, including damages and both lots of costs. As part of the £0.5 million, Allied took from the Company the surplus warehouse, (the old copperworks), which cost the Company £60k, at a value of £150k, the price the

1979 – John Townend with the background of the House of Commons.

Company had it on the market for; John had some satisfaction that they couldn't sell it and accepted £75k three years later. The other laugh was that, although the Willerby Manor was a subsidiary of the Company, Allied, for some reason, never realised the hotel was part of the family's wealth.

Before the case was lost in the House of Lords, John had contingency plans just in case the case was lost. The formulation of Keeling's was changed to make it a spirit-based drink, but to maintain its financial viability it was necessary to reduce the strength. Once the Court case was lost a spirit-based Keeling's was rapidly launched, on which the Company had to pay the spirit duty. In addition to dropping the strength, margins had also to be cut and the price increased and the advertising budget slashed. These measures, together with the adverse publicity of the Court case, meant sales started a long decline, which in the end continued and resulted in production in Hull ceasing and buying from a Dutch Advocaat produced in Holland. Eventually it was taken off the market.

So ended the Keeling's Saga; if the case had been won it would have meant that Townend's were 'into the big time'. Losing could have bankrupted the Company. It didn't, but it cast a shadow over the Company for a good ten years. John always felt the decision was wrong as it stopped innovation and product development. He often mused, if it had been an innovative French firm that had been taken to court in France or a Dutch firm in Holland, would the foreign court have found in favour of the English Company – hardly likely!

Chapter 13:

Pubs, Restaurants and Hotels

Three of the four public houses bought by the Company in Charles' time had been sold but the Nag's Head, alongside the main Beverley/Bridlington Road remained. It was tenanted to Alec Townend for a number of years but it came back into management in 1969 and, with the somewhat reckless enthusiasm of youth, John decided he would like to go into the restaurant business. In 1970 he got planning permission to build a large 120-cover restaurant onto the existing pub. He intended to turn it into an upmarket road house with excellent food. However, he didn't have a clue about the restaurant business and as the extension neared completion he suddenly realised he had a problem. By chance he happened to give a lift home, after the Humberside Round Table, to a fellow member, Derek Baugh. He had been trained as a chef at the Dorchester Hotel, London, and after a number of jobs as a chef, he had made a career change of direction and went into education. He was at that time working as a senior lecturer in catering at Hull Technical College. John started telling him about his plans for the Nag's Head, when Derek said, 'I'm disillusioned and bored to death working in education. Compared to what I did in industry I'm only working half time and when I try to help the students by working longer hours the rest of the staff get difficult and give me the cold shoulder.' When John said that, if it was a success, he intended to open up other catering premises and build up a catering side to the House of Townend, Derek said he would be interested in joining John. They discussed John's plans and arranged to meet the following week to discuss their ideas in detail.

As a result the Townend Catering Company was set up, originally to operate the Nag's Head but with a hope that there would be other establishments following on. With Derek Baugh as the resident Managing Director and John as Chairman, this was the start of a very successful partnership that was to last some 18 years. They were two young men in a hurry. The building of the restaurant, as always in such contracts, ran late and it was completed early in December. They rushed to open in time for the Christmas trade; this turned out to be a big mistake as Derek offered high-class à la carte cuisine. The wastage to start with was naturally high and double time was paid over the Christmas period to the staff. After the first three months the accounts showed a thumping loss. John remembers saying to Derek at the first Board Meeting, 'We can forget any thoughts of expanding until we get this place right.' Derek worked very hard and after about 18 months the Nag's Head became quite profitable and established a reputation as one of the best eating places in the East Riding.

In 1974 Derek went to see John and said, 'The Nag's Head is going well but you must appreciate I didn't join you just to run a pub/restaurant for the rest of my life. I would like to find somewhere where we can move into banqueting in a big way.' By coincidence another member of the Humberside Round Table, Dudley Moore of Dutton Moore Chartered Accountants, was acting for the Hotel Eden, which was owned three ways by a builder called Scruton, his son and Tom Farmer, who was the resident manager. Dudley approached John to see if he was interested in purchasing this hotel. John remembers very well he and Derek going to Dudley's office to negotiate with the Scruton's.

John believed the reason for the sale was that the partners had fallen out and so he took a pretty tough line. It paid off and after a couple hours of haggling, they bought the hotel for £150k. John then had the problem of going back and telling his father, who was still the Chairman and was unaware of the negotiations. He nearly had a heart attack! The deal was completed in July 1974. John always maintained this was the most important decision in his business career. When he lost the Keeling's case the collateral of the hotel was important for the banks, who had to loan a large sum to pay costs and damages. In addition, when the retail business was in serious decline and losing money, it was the hotel's profits that kept the Company going while it was restructured and changed from being principally a retailer to mainly a wholesaler.

It is interesting that prior to becoming the Hotel Eden the building was actually called the Willerby Manor and

Willerby Manor Hotel.

had been a private residence occupied by a well-known hotelier, Freddy Gamble, who owned Powolny's, the White House Hotel and the New York Hotel. When John was a young man, the New York Hotel had the cream of the East Yorkshire banqueting business, just as the Willerby Manor has the cream of the business today. Freddie was a real character and lived there with his wife and his mistress as a ménage à trois. While this would not cause comment in the permissive era we now live in, one can imagine the twitterings there were in Hull just after the war. Freddie's wild parties, to which visiting theatricals were invited, were legendary.

Under Derek, however, nothing untoward ever went on. John remembers Derek telling him that one local hotel, which shall remain nameless, had a much better room occupancy than ours. This surprised him because it was not nearly as good as the Manor. Derek told him it was because they used to let rooms during the afternoons to businessmen with their secretaries or girlfriends and then re-let them in the evening to normal guests. As an accountant, John thought this was a splendid utilisation of assets but Derek insisted it would ruin the family's reputation. In view of the fact that John later went into politics with all the ensuing problems of sleaze, Derek's advice was very good. One could imagine the headlines in the tabloid press, 'MP runs hotel of ill repute'!

Unfortunately, Mr. Scruton, being a builder, insisted on keeping some outbuildings and half the main lawn and some unused land at the rear, on which he hoped to obtain planning permission to build. Mr. Scruton senior was also living in a flat in the hotel and he insisted on at least a three-year lease. Having bought the hotel from builders Derek and John assumed that all the additions that had been made would be of the highest standard. How wrong they were. They have never stopped spending on the building since they bought it. The flat roof caused continuous problems until it was replaced with a pitched roof, the floors creaked and were not soundproof and a considerable amount of money was spent to overcome this problem. Only 18 of the 30 bedrooms had en-suite bathrooms and the decorations in the whole building were fairly grotty. Another

disadvantage was that the ballroom was on several levels to give it the atmosphere of a nightclub where you could have floorshows but was completely impractical for large-scale banqueting.

For John and Derek to achieve their objectives, the property clearly needed large amounts of investment for improvements and expansion. Investment started almost immediately and has continued up to the present day. Derek wanted to build up a reputation in large scale, high-quality banqueting so the first investment was a complete revamp of the ballroom. The floor was levelled and new windows installed together with new lighting and a sound system. The hotel did not have a good reputation and so it was decided to change the name to the Willerby Manor Hotel, the name of the company which owned the Eden. A manager was installed in the Nag's Head under Derek's control.

The catering company now had two units and the following year, 1975, John bought an old bank adjacent to Thomas Brothers, his subsidiary in Elland. It was a lovely old building and it was decided to convert it into one of the new wine bars with food which were sweeping London at the time. Much of the décor and furnishings of the establishment were done by Jennifer, John's wife, who for many years has dealt with the decorations and soft furnishings in the hotel. The catering company now had three establishments; it was a testing time for Derek. We knew he was excellent at running one property but had he the management expertise to run a chain? – only time would tell.

One of the problems at the Willerby Manor was that future development would be restricted by the size of the site. In 1976 an opportunity arose when 90 Main Street, a house with a substantial garden, came on the market. Its garden backed onto the hotel and came right alongside the kitchen; there was only a narrow footpath from the car park to the kitchen. The house was auctioned and John instructed their agents to buy it, which they did. Most of the garden was fenced and incorporated into the hotel grounds and Derek moved from the Manager's house, adjoining the bedroom block, into 90 Main Street. This left the old house available for alternative use. In December 1979 planning permission was granted to build an extra storey onto the Manager's house and convert the house into bedrooms; this resulted in another six en-suite bedrooms. Just before the project was completed, the Chairman, Charles, died in 1977. Dorothy, his widow, was frightened of continuing to live alone after an unfortunate incident and so a flat was made out of two of the new bedrooms, which consisted of a bedroom, sitting room, bathroom and kitchen.

From the very start John and Derek had ambitious plans for the long-term development of the site. In 1978 they applied for Outline Planning Permission for extra hotel accommodation, swimming pool, squash courts and car parking. In 1979 full planning permission was granted. Unfortunately, the loss of the Keeling's case and the large amount of cost and damages put paid to such a large-scale development, which had to be postponed for many a year. However, investment continued on a more modest scale and in 1980 planning permission was granted for a kitchen extension and improvements at a cost of £27k.

It was felt that there was no future for a hotel like the Willerby Manor unless all its rooms had en-suite bathrooms. It was decided a programme of conversions should be commenced, even though some rooms would be lost. This scheme was completed by 1982 at a cost of £42k less a grant from the Tourist Board of £7,200. In 1981 the hotel was able to acquire the half of the lawn which had been retained by Scruton's. The lease of Mr. Scruton senior's flat had run out. He wanted to stay but from the hotel's point of view it was beneficial to turn his flat into more letting bedrooms. John, however, had another idea, which was important for the long-term benefit of the hotel. He told Mr. Scruton he would renew his lease if he would sell us the part of the garden that he had retained. A purchase price of £8k was agreed and the hotel was able to maintain the integrity of the garden, which was a vital asset.

The loss of the Keeling's case resulted in a pressure on cash to pay the costs and damages, so when in 1981 the Company received an approach from a prospective purchaser to buy the Nag's Head at a very good price the Board had to seriously consider it. Since Derek had moved to Willerby Manor the Nag's Head's profits had declined and it was decided to sell. The next year there was an approach from someone interested in the Elland Wine Bar, which had never been as successful as had been hoped, so the offer was accepted. Derek's strengths were clearly in running one good place rather than a chain and so John decided that in future they would put all the cash available for investment into the hotel rather than looking for another establishment. In 1986 John sold 15 of his wine shops and decided to invest the proceeds in developing the hotel site. First, in 1986 he built a large wine market alongside the kitchen; the site had previously been part of the garden of 90 Main Street.

Derek Baugh said at the time, 'If it's not a success, it'll make a super function suite as it is immediately adjacent to the kitchen.' Derek had never achieved his aim that the Willerby Manor should be the best restaurant in the area and so, after a succession of head chefs, he decided that instead of managing from front of house he would go into the kitchen and become a Chef/Patron, which was the formula of many top French establishments. This was a great success, the quality of the food improved dramatically and the restaurant took off and was frequently completely booked up. The maximum number of tables was squashed in.

The restaurant had no outside windows and Derek felt we would never get the recognition from the Guides that the food deserved until we had a much more luxurious restaurant. Terry Glazebrook, a designer from Scarborough, was appointed to plan and design a development plan for the property. Phase 1 was to have a large extension to the ballroom to accommodate up to 400 diners, a new bar, and a larger restaurant. The existing ballroom bar was knocked into the restaurant, doubling its size. It now included its own bar for pre-dinner drinks within the restaurant area and had a magnificent view of the gardens. The ballroom included new toilets, a large bar, separate entrance and its own car park. This improved facility meant that the Willerby Manor would be able to accommodate the largest functions in the area.

It was a large investment and its success depended upon Derek. John knew Derek, encouraged by his new wife, was toying with the idea of buying his own place.

He tried to head off the possibility by offering to give Derek 10% of the equity of the Willerby Manor. John wanted to tie him in for ten years so the gift was subject to a provision that if Derek left within ten years the Company could buy back the shares at par. Originally Derek accepted this offer and the matter was put in the solicitor's hands. However, there was the inevitable delay one gets from lawyers and, before it was signed in 1977, Derek decided he didn't want to be tied down for ten years and he found a property that he could convert to a restaurant with rooms. This decision came like a bolt from the blue and was really bad news for John as the investment was two-thirds completed. After losing the Keeling's case, the death of his Production Director and the retirement of his MD he was badly stretched and he was still in Parliament. In one blow he was losing not only his Managing Director but also his Head Chef. Clearly with his reputation, Derek would attract a lot of restaurant customers and it would take a lot longer to get an adequate return on the investment. Although John was saddened by the event, as one who passionately believed in individual enterprise he understood the reasons and was delighted at Derek's success at the Walkington Manor Hotel.

When Derek left, John seriously wondered whether he should sell the hotel. However, the Manor had become part of the Townend family and two of the children, against his advice, decided that they wanted to go into the hotel business, so he decided to soldier on and advertise for a Director/Manager. Robert Wade was appointed MD and did quite a good job. The restaurant never returned to the popularity it achieved under Derek but the new, enlarged banqueting suite was the best in the area and the hotel attracted the large functions. Robert Wade achieved a satisfactory level of profit. In January 1988 Paul Bocuse, one of France's most famous chefs, came over and performed the opening ceremony of the new Lafite Restaurant. Just one month later the hotel received a RAC Merit Award. In the same year Dorothy Townend died and her apartment was converted to two en-suite rooms. In 1989 the Company took the opportunity to sell 90 Main Street and the proceeds received helped finance the investment programme.

The second phase of the development plan had been agreed and was awaiting implementation when Robert Wade left. He was replaced by Howard Fradley, who arrived just in time to see the work started. It included complete revamping of the Reception area; the Cocktail Bar was extended into the garden in the form of a conservatory to create Everglades, an all-day restaurant. The total investment was £200k.

Howard Fradley's period was not a happy one and he left in 1991. Whilst in charge he brought back François, who had been a very successful Restaurant Manager under Derek Baugh. He was a good front of house man and it was decided to give François a chance and put him in charge with the title Director and General Manager. Because he didn't have the administrative skills required it was decided that Alexandra Townend, who was working as Deputy Manager at the Dedham Vale Hotel, should be brought back as Deputy GM with particular responsibility for such matters as administration and costing. John had always been opposed to Alexandra going into the hospitality industry for a career as he thought that, due to the antisocial hours, it was not a very good career for a bright young girl. However, Alexandra was extremely focused and determined, she knew exactly what she wanted to do and she persuaded her father to let her work in the hotel during school holidays.

It soon became patently obvious to everyone, including John, that she was set on a career in the industry and when her schooling finished she enrolled at Westminster Hotel School in London. Three years later she had graduated with an HND in Hotel Catering and Institutional Management. As part of the course she had spent six months in the Boulestin Restaurant in Covent Garden, working her way around every aspect of the business. She was the first woman ever to work in the kitchen at this well-known restaurant. Following graduation she didn't, as many people had thought, opt to join the family business immediately. She was invited to join the Gerry Milsom Group in Colchester, a successful family business, on which she had based her dissertation at college. Alexandra spent 2½ years with the Milsom Group, joining initially as PA to the

Directors. This, combined with working in their Tollbooth Restaurant in Dedham, gave her the management grooming she was looking for. Following promotion she spent 18 months as Deputy Manager of the Dedham Vale Hotel.

Shortly after taking over, François employed David Roberts, who had left the Manor on two previous occasions to become a Number One, but events had not worked out as he would have wished. This was an excellent opportunity for the hotel and it was an astute move by David, who realised François would probably not stay. To overcome staff problems François employed a lot of French, both in the restaurant and in the kitchen. The gamble did not work as Alexandra and François did not see eye to eye and there were aspects of his management with which she disagreed.

It soon became clear that they could not work together and Alexandra said she would leave and go back south. Jennifer wisely pointed out to John that if she once went she probably would never return. A family business only survives and continues if some members of the family are able and willing to carry on. The matter came to a head when François announced that he was leaving. Alexandra was only 22 and it was thought she was a bit young for the total responsibility. So, David Roberts was asked if he would be prepared to be Joint General Manager with Alexandra, with a seat on the Board. During the three periods he had worked with the Company he knew the business inside out. David, surprisingly, said he would rather not. He said, 'Twice I left to be a Number One and it didn't work out. I am quite happy to be Number Two to Alex and support her where I can.' Alex was, therefore, appointed Director and General Manager and David was appointed Deputy General Manager with a seat on the Board.

When François left, the French staff closed ranks in support of their fellow countryman. They set about making life difficult for Alex. One evening quite late she rang up her father, almost in tears, saying, 'They are trying to sabotage the business.' Her father asked her what she meant and she replied, 'We had a full restaurant last night and the French Head Chef decided to "go slow". By 10.00 pm only three tables had been served.'

She added, 'He will destroy the business. Can I fire him?' 'No,' he said. 'Certainly not, I will not allow anybody to destroy my business. I am going to have the pleasure of sacking him myself.' First thing the next morning he got into his car, drove to the hotel and fired him immediately. As you can imagine, the word went round the building like wildfire. A few minutes later the French Restaurant Manager asked to see John. He was on a monthly contract but he came in and said, 'I am going to leave on Wednesday' – that was four days before Christmas. John said, 'You won't leave on Wednesday.' He replied, 'I will and you can't stop me.' John said, 'I can. You will leave today and I will have you escorted off the premises now.' The French chef had a French girlfriend, who was also on the staff, and so she decided to leave immediately. John told them they had to vacate their rooms in the hotel the following day. He was rather amused when that afternoon he received a phone call from the chef's girlfriend's father, who turned out to be a rather important businessman in France, complaining that he had sacked his daughter without notice. John explained to him that he had not sacked his daughter at all. She had walked out. 'Ah, but,' he said, 'you sacked her boyfriend, who she is living with, so that is the same thing.' This is just another example of how the French mind works differently from the English.

The remaining English staff, who had not been very happy at the large number of French, who tended to be cliquey, really came up trumps. Their attitude was, 'We are not going to let the French ruin this business and destroy our jobs.' They got stuck in, worked long hours and kept the ship afloat. David Roberts' value as a trained chef came to the fore immediately; he took his jacket off, went into the kitchen and took control. With David in the kitchen, Alexandra went into the restaurant and acted as Restaurant Manager. The hotel survived and Alexandra won her Waterloo. John's family maintained that his Euro scepticism became much stronger as a result of this event.

The whole affair did give Alexandra her first publicity as Managing Director – someone leaked what had happened to the *Hull Daily Mail* and the headline on its front page read, 'Allo, Allo and Au Revoir – French staff walk out on MP's daughter'. They did a great hatchet job on Alexandra. Not for the first time she realised the disadvantage of having a father who was an MP whom the press loved to hate. It is said, 'All publicity is good publicity', but on that occasion Alexandra would not agree.

Many in the business community thought John had gone stark raving mad by putting such a young girl in charge and, due to her being small in stature, she actually looked younger than she was. They thought it would end in disaster. What did surprise many people was that John had a reputation as a male chauvinist, who was Politically Incorrect as far as the female sex was concerned. In the hotel business there are three things that reduce profits – wastage, excessive costs and fiddling. Alexandra set about all three like a terrier, to such an effect that she doubled the profits in the first year.

John had taken a big gamble but he believed that his children should get responsibility whilst relatively young and, if they proved not to have the necessary ability to succeed, the sooner he knew the better so that the business could be sold. This was a searing experience for Alexandra but she rose to the challenge, helped very much by David. This experience certainly put steel into her and as a result she became a better manager. After a year in the job Alexandra became so successful that she was appointed Managing Director at the age of only 23. She also received an Acorn Award, a National Award given each year to the 30 young people under the age of 30 most likely to succeed in the hospitality industry. One of Alexandra's first projects was to close Raphael's, the pasta/pizza restaurant, which had run out of steam. There was some discussion as to what the vacant space should be used for and Jennifer suggested that the Wine Market should move into the smaller but attractive space which had been occupied by Raphael's and that the hotel would take over the Wine Market's building and turn it into another banqueting suite for 150. John and Alex agreed. This new suite was named The Talbot and became a very successful addition to the banqueting facilities.

Alexandra Townend, Managing Director of Willerby Manor.

A few years before Alexandra joined the Company, John had been approached by an estate agent, acting for the owners of a disused market garden which ran from Main Street behind the houses on Well Lane to the Willerby Manor car park. They wanted to develop this land but the planners would not allow access for a mini estate onto Well Lane, so they could only develop it if they could get the Willerby Manor to allow access through its land. They were prepared to discuss various possibilities — buying an access or doing a joint development. They offered quite generous terms but John rejected these because he didn't want more houses built near the hotel with an increase in complaints for noise. The owners were left with a derelict piece of land with no planning permission. They wanted to sell and they made another approach; the price they asked for was reasonable but John managed to negotiate a lower price and bought it for the family. Planning permission was obtained for a block of four town houses fronting onto Main Street. John gave a plot to each of his four children and he then built four houses, financed mostly by mortgages; subsequently, Alexandra and her brother, John Charles, each occupied one. James' house was let with the idea that, if he came back to work for the Company, he would have a house. The fourth house was used for the Manager after 90 Main Street had been sold. The balance of the land was to be held for future hotel expansion.

By 1994, although the hotel was fairly profitable the room occupancy was not very high and it was felt that more and more customers were booking into hotels that offered the facility of a swimming pool and health club. It was always John's ambition that the Willerby Manor should be the best hotel in the area and he had always been prepared to invest. He had intended to build a swimming pool ever since the hotel had been purchased. Originally it had been intended to adjoin the bedroom block, but it was now decided that it would be better to site the health club on the land purchased from the market garden and build another bedroom block of 18 rooms adjoining the existing bedroom block. Plans were drawn up and planning permission was applied for. Although the Planning Officers did not object to the scheme, the Company, not for the first or the last time, suffered from political opposition on the Committee from the majority Liberal group. The planning permission was turned down for what could only be political reasons – that John was a Conservative MP. The Council cited only one reason and that was that the development would attract too much traffic onto the site.

As the hotel already had planning permission for a health club adjoining the bedroom block, this seemed a nonsense. The Company architect said that, as the existing planning permission would generate the same traffic as the new one, the grounds for objection would not stand up if the hotel went to appeal. The Planning Officer rang up Alexandra to discuss the Committee's decision and she asked him, 'Does this refusal mean that if we want a health club we will have to build it at the other end of the site?' 'What do you mean?' he asked, 'Well, we already have a Planning Permission for there and we renewed it only two years ago,' said Alexandra. 'Oh my God!' he said. 'The Planners had forgotten that permission had been granted and had not informed the Committee.' He knew they would lose on appeal with costs so he had to go back to the Committee and advise them that they had no alternative other than to pass it, which subsequently they did.

Tony Watts was appointed the architect and drew up detailed plans. Before these were finalised, John, Alexandra, John Charles and Jennifer visited a considerable number of health clubs around the country to obtain ideas to incorporate in the Willerby Manor scheme. They had one question that they asked at every place they visited, which proved invaluable. 'If you were going to build your health club again what changes would you make, based on your experience?' It was remarkable how many problems had arisen after the building was completed. In nearly every case they came back and the plans were amended. The final plan was considerably different from the one produced by the architect, but the Directors were pretty certain that they had foreseen all the problems. John then approached the bank and negotiated a loan to cover 100% of the cost of the scheme. The job went out to tender and Quibell's were awarded the contract at a price of approximately £1.4 million; work commenced early in 1996.

Alexandra decided she would take on the task of project management. She did it brilliantly. Most contractors make their money by charging high prices for extras. Alexandra decided that was not going to happen with the Willerby Manor so she informed the contractors that 'no bills for extras would be accepted unless they had been priced and accepted by her before the work began'. She was like a little terrier; every day she walked round the site with a clipboard making notes of any work with which she wasn't satisfied. She had developed a very good relationship with the owner of the swimming pool firm, who tipped her off when he saw any of the contractors trying to cut corners. With this close supervision she got under the skin of the Site Manager. One day he said, 'The trouble with you, Miss Townend, is that your standards are too high.' Alexandra, as quick as a flash, replied, 'When we gave you the contract it wasn't on the basis that we would get a low standard job!' When the project was being planned it was agreed that what was wanted was a high-quality job with low maintenance costs. This probably cost an extra £50k but it was worth every penny. When the project was finished it was widely acknowledged that the Health Club with its 20-metre swimming pool and well equipped gymnasium was the most upmarket in the area. The opening of the Health Club was well received and membership quickly reached 1,000.

The new 18-room bedroom block was also built to a very high standard; the rooms were larger and many up to mini-suite standard. Bathrooms and finishes were to a high standard. A number of the larger rooms were dual purpose – Meeting Rooms during the day, and in the evening, with pull-down beds and pull-out bedside tables, they became bedrooms. The effect of this quality development on the hotel was considerable. The general view in the area was that the hotel had moved up into a different league. Before the development, the room occupancy rate had been in the mid-40% range. It immediately jumped to 60%, including the new rooms, and has continued to rise until it reached almost 80%.

Chapter 14:

The Agency Business

The development of the Keeling's brand had resulted in a sales team consisting of the Sales Director, Jim Moggridge, and four salesmen. This was quite a large overhead and, when the future of Keeling's was at risk, through litigation, it was felt that the salesmen should be selling other products.

It was agreed that the Company would look around for exclusive agencies for importing wines into the UK. The first opportunity arose in 1975 when there was an advertisement in the trade press from Wisdom & Warter, sherry producers, which was owned by the Gonzalez family of Tio Pepe fame. They had supplied their brand as the main sherry to Augustus Barnett, a large and growing national chain of cut-price wine shops. Wisdom & Warter had got an export licence for 60,000 cases, which had been bottled and were ready for shipment when out of the blue Barnett's cancelled the order and went to another sherry producer. This left Wisdom & Warter with a surplus stock of 60,000 cases. Sherry prices had recently been increased but, having an existing export licence at the old price, they could offer the stock at a very competitive rate.

John spotted the advert and suggested to Jim Moggridge that there might be an opportunity to buy a large parcel for the reps to sell alongside Keeling's. Jim said we should buy all the 60,000 cases or none. If we bought the lot we would control the selling price. Contact was made with Wisdom & Water. They had had a number of enquiries to buy parts of this parcel but had not made any decisions. John and Jim decided they should fly out immediately, so they told Wisdom & Warter not to make a decision on the enquiries until they got to Jerez. Jaime Gonzalez, Chairman of Wisdom & Warter, and Antonio Arias were impressed with the speed of Townend's reaction. The deal was done by which Townend's bought the whole consignment and Wisdom & Warter handed over all the enquiries they had received. John wanted them to appoint the House of Townend as the sole agent for the UK market but Jaime said he was not prepared to take a decision at that stage. Clearly he had reservations about appointing a Hull firm as opposed to a London firm as his agent. With a very competitive price, Townend's quickly started making inroads to the sherry market, supplying Cash and Carry's, supermarkets, wholesalers and brewers. Morrisons became one of the biggest buyers. Jaime was impressed and, when the 60,000 cases were sold, he appointed the House of Townend as his agent.

In seeking other agencies, the problem John came up against time and time again was that they were a firm from 'Hull'. He and Jim had to do a big selling job, convincing the brand owners that their enthusiasm, financial soundness and integrity offset the lack of prestige by not having a London-based operation. Instead of negotiating by letter and telephone, John and Jim would jump on a plane and visit the target company. They had some success but they never got a household name. An agency was acquired for 'Peralada' Spanish wines, which became well known in the famous Spanish 'Champagne' case, and for a range of Italian wines from Vino del Piave.

The division made good progress until 1979 when as a result of the court case the Keeling's recipe had to be changed and the profitability of the brand dropped dramatically. Keeling's had underpinned the cost of the sales force and eventually the sales didn't justify a sales force so large. It was decided to abandon the small customers and let the Sales Director deal with the large customers on the 20/80 philosophy. It became clear that this policy was not succeeding as hoped because Jim Moggridge preferred organising others rather than spending most of his time on the road negotiating with the buyers of the big groups, which he was good at. A young wife and daughter influenced his desire not to travel nationally. In 1983, therefore, he left and started his own business in Hull, competing with the Company for local wholesale trade and retail customers. He was replaced by Philip Barty, a very enthusiastic and personable young man. During his stay, he and John visited Portugal and obtained the agency for the Solar brand. He eventually left in 1987 and, like Jim

Moggridge, set up his own company in partnership with a friend.

John, although in Parliament, took over the two biggest, remaining Keeling's accounts, which were Safeway and International Stores, and he would personally go down annually and negotiate the price for the following year. After the loss of the case, Keeling's lost its price advantage and the Company couldn't afford television advertising, so it became a secondary brand,

John Charles Townend.

sold purely on the basis of price. It was John's experience, dealing personally with these two customers, that made him eventually decide to abandon the agency business supplying Cash & Carry's, supermarkets and multiples, where the business was large but the margin minute and you could be in one year and out the next. With the sales of Keeling's dropping, Wisdom & Warter's sherry became the most important brand. With the departure of Jim Moggridge and Philip Barty the Company was temporarily without a Sales Director and Wisdom & Warter had serious concerns about their UK sales agent. Jaime and Antonio were coming over to London and asked for a meeting. John's son, John Charles, had joined the Company the previous year and was learning the business. By a stroke of luck the Company received an enquiry for sherry from a medium-sized supermarket group called Low Cost. As there was nobody available to visit them, young John Charles went off to see them; to his father's delight he returned with the contract to supply them with their main sherry. This was a great coup for the fourth generation. It also meant that Townend's had some good positive news to tell the Wisdom & Warter team. John wrote a paper on a marketing programme for Wisdom & Water sherry for the UK markets. Father and son discussed the tactics they should use; they decided that John Charles would present the paper as his.

The meeting took place in John's London flat. John took control of the meeting from the start so that initially Wisdom & Warter had no chance to express their reservations about continuing to allow Townend's to be their agents. He introduced son John Charles, the fourth generation who had recently joined the Company, to Wisdom & Warter and informed them he was a graduate of Warwick University Business School, about his training in the industry for a year in France and Germany, and informed them of the new, large customer that John Charles had secured. John Charles then presented his paper brilliantly, according to his proud father. His marketing degree and training had obviously had some effect. After he had finished, John urged them to back this young man, who was 'going places'. Jaime Gonzalez was impressed and agreed to continue the

agency, after which they admitted that when they walked through the door they intended to terminate the agreement and part company with the House of Townend.

With the increasing penetration of the UK market by southern hemisphere wine producers, Townend's had fallen behind because it was overwhelmingly European-based. One of the great success stories was Chile, but Townend's seemed to have missed the boat. In 1988 out of the blue Robert Walker, Fiona Townend's father-in-law, who had been doing consultancy work with a large Chilean conglomerate, found that they owned a winery with a well-known brand, Santa Rita. When one of their directors visited the UK Robert asked John if he would like to meet him. John was interested and invited them both to dinner at the House of Commons. Santa Rita was already represented in the UK market but situations change and, if the relationship broke up, John wanted them to think of the House of Townend as an alternative partner. John got on very well with the Chilean gentleman, who, when he returned to Chile, persuaded the Chilean Wine Trade Organisation to invite John to join a high-powered delegation from the UK to visit Chile and see ten of the top wine producers.

The other invitees included Robert Joseph, the well-known wine writer; Oz Clarke, wine writer and TV pundit, the Chief Buyer of Victoria Wine and Manuel Moreno, Santa Rita's agent. The cream of Chilean wine producers were visited and some excellent wines tasted. John realised Chilean wine was going to be big and that Townend's must get an agency. Unfortunately, all the estates visited had already appointed UK agents. John got quite friendly with the man from the Chilean Wine Trade Association, who had organised the visit and he promised to let John know if he heard any whispers of any producer being disaffected with his agent who could provide an opening for Townend's.

Some time after John returned from the trip he was approached out of the blue by a young man, (whom I will call 'X'), the son of a former colleague, to see if he was interested in importing Chilean wines produced by Professor Alejandro (Alex) Hernández, whom he had got to know when he was a university student. Alex was

Professor of Viticulture and Viniculture at Santiago University but owned a couple of vineyards as a sideline, where he put his theories into practice. He asked 'X', who was returning to England, if he could find a UK importer. John was very interested and asked to see samples. He stipulated that, if the quality and price were right, the House of Townend would only take it if they were given the exclusive agency. The samples arrived. The white was pretty poor but the red, a Cabernet Sauvignon, was pretty good. 'X' told John that Alex was shortly going to visit the UK and could a meeting be arranged; he also asked if a deal was struck could there be a job in it for him. John said a decision on that would depend upon his son, John Charles, who was progressively taking over the day-to-day running of the business. John invited 'X' and the Professor to have dinner with him and his son at the House of Commons to discuss a deal.

A few weeks before the visit 'X' rang John and said he had decided to take the agency himself, so the dinner was cancelled. John was a little surprised as 'X' had had no business experience, no office or infrastructure and he couldn't see how he would be able to handle such a project. He knew it would all end in tears. He did not have the address of the winery so he wrote to his contact in Chile, explained the situation and asked if he could let him have the Professor's address because he wanted to write informing him of Townend's history and the fact that, if at any time in the future he wasn't happy with his UK agent and wanted to change, Townend's would be interested. Whilst awaiting a reply from his Chilean contact John was surprised to receive a letter direct from Professor Hernández saying that he had been speaking with John's contact and was surprised to hear what had happened. He said that no way would he entrust the sale of his wine in the UK to an inexperienced young man just out of university and he would very much like to discuss with Townend's the question of their taking the agency for the UK.

Townend's had missed the boat on so many New World wines and were now looking round for the next country where wines would suddenly hit the UK market. They decided that Argentina was a possibility and that they should make a visit there, assess the wine industry and look for suitable producers whom they might like to represent in the UK market. The trip was all planned when the letter from Alex arrived and they decided that at the end of their Argentinian trip they would fly to Chile to see him before coming home. When the Townend's arrived in Argentina they found there had been practically no visits of English wine merchants since the Falklands War, so they were certainly ahead of the field. At that stage the proud Argentinian winemakers were not prepared to accept criticism or suggestions as to how their wines could be improved. They travelled widely to Mendoza and to Salta in the Cafayate Valley in the far north and visited the head offices of several large wine companies in Buenos Aires.

Whilst in Buenos Aires, John Charles relates an incident when his father's diplomacy was again on full show. Bear in mind that diplomatic relations had only just been restored between Britain and Argentina, following the Falklands conflict. When visiting the Cafayate producer, Etchart, in their offices in Buenos Aires, John Charles was getting very irritated that the Argentinians were somewhat uninterested in getting down to talking serious business. The problem was that the boss of the company was one of the business advisors to the Argentinian President, Carlos Menem. All he wanted to do was talk politics with John. The hours went by and soon the two Townend's were being royally entertained at the Argentinian Jockey Club. In the very impressive surroundings, the party of six – John, John Charles, the company's boss and his three henchmen, ate and drank quite happily until the cheese course arrived, when the Etchart boss could restrain himself no longer. 'John,' he said. Silence engulfed the rest of the table. 'Can I ask you a question?' John replied, 'Yes, of course, you can, but I can't promise you will like the answer.' 'No, no, of course, but what do the British people really think about us, the Argentinians, because of the Falklands'war?' All around stopped what they were eating and looked; John Charles held his breath; John carried on munching his cheese crackers and answered without a moment's thought 'Oh, no problem. Why should there be? After all, we won!'

In the end they took two agencies, one from the family firm of Michel Torino in Salta and one from a subsidiary of Moët & Chandon, Proviar. They were too early; the wines did not take off in the UK and Michel Torino went broke during one of Argentina's successive financial crises. The Proviar wines were subsequently dropped.

The visit to Chile was much more successful. The Townend's were met by Alex at Santiago airport and he took them to visit his estates, Portal del Alto. One was the most beautiful vineyards they had ever visited; it was situated in the foothills of the Andes. They tasted the wine. The red Cabernet Sauvignon was excellent, just what they were looking for; they then tasted the white. It was pretty awful. John said he was very worried that to get the agency they would have to take both wines. Alex asked him what he thought. He replied, a little diffidently, 'Not very good and not really acceptable for the quality end of the market in which we specialise.' John was relieved and delighted when Alex said, 'You are quite right. I would have been disappointed if you had said anything else. I am an expert in producing first-class fruit. To make good red wine all you need is good fruit, a good barrel and lots of know-how. To make good white wines you need a lot of expensive equipment, which I don't have. But as I make money in the red, I will invest and it will get better.' It did and within three years Townend's started importing the wine into the UK. The negotiation ended successfully and Townend's returned with the sole agency for the UK. The agency is the only one in the original portfolio that has survived into the centenary year of the Company. Alex is now semi-retired, like John, and his son has taken over.

During the discussions, Alex told John that he was quite annoyed with 'X', who before leaving Chile had offered to help him find a UK agent and had never told Alex about his approaching Townend's and the subsequent discussions and the invitation to dine at the House of Commons. This agreement had some surprising repercussions. Some time after John had returned to Westminster he received a vitriolic letter from 'X's' mother, accusing him of acting dishonourably to her son and stealing the agency from under his nose.

She said she had written to the Chief Whip and Sir Cranley Onslow, the Chairman of the 1922 Committee, complaining of his behaviour. Sir Cranley sent her a dusty reply with a copy to John, saying this was purely a business matter and nothing to do with the 1922 Committee or the Conservative Party. If the Chief Whip, Tim Renton, had taken the same line that would have been the end of the matter, but he did not. John was summoned to his office and, before he could say a word, Renton called him 'a shit' and accused him of stealing the agency off 'X' and preventing a young man getting a start in life.

John was furious at being verbally attacked and a shouting match ensued which ended with John walking out. He went back to his office and wrote out a full account of what had happened and sent it to Tim Renton and demanded a further interview. This took place a week later in Renton's office. He was clearly not interested in John's account of what happened. John demanded an apology for being insulted by Renton, who refused. John walked out saying that until he got an apology the Whips could not count on his support in the lobbies. He went on a voting strike. His Whip was a Midlander, and as John refused to give in the weeks slipped by. He pleaded with him. 'You must remember,' he said, 'we're both straight talking, provincial businessmen. We think differently to these southern Etonians.' Then the penny dropped. Tim Renton, 'X' and his father were all Etonians. John never got his apology. After six weeks something came up that affected his beloved constituency, Bridlington, so John voted. But the two men never spoke again. No doubt another nail was driven in John's political career.

When Philip Barty left, only one representative remained, Keith Bates, but he left shortly after John Charles joined the Company in 1988. John Charles was really thrown in the deep end. There was nobody to look after what was left of the national sales customers for 18 months until Eric Parker joined in 1989 as National Sales Manager.

John Charles did a jolly good cost-effective job and was quite successful with Wisdom & Warter's sherry. His great initial successes were Lowcost, Bookers and

Budgens. Eric Parker was an older man who had a good reputation in the trade with supposedly lots of contacts. One thing he did bring was a connection with Caronne Ste. Gemme, a good quality, well priced Bordeaux. In the same year as Eric joined, John Charles had negotiated the agency for Bodegas Lan Rioja. Whilst Eric was Sales Manager he and John Charles obtained the agency for Cellier des Dauphin Rhône wine, a leading brand in France. Unfortunately his sales did not warrant his cost; reluctantly it was decided he would have to go.

John Charles once more decided to look after the handful of big remaining customers, including LowCost, Bookers and Budgens. But he had some considerable success; he persuaded Morrisons to make Wisdom & Warter their main fighting brand of sherry and he also got Wisdom's into the Co-op and Cellier des Dauphins into Makro. Although he had only seven or eight big customers, the volume was fairly big and in 1993 the National Sales Division, with no salesmen to pay, was making a good contribution. John Charles was doing very well in running the business and his father, who was away at Westminster, decided that he should be made Managing Director. John Charles said that, despite his success, he felt that in dealing with such big companies the business was built on sand. The buyers were very aggressive and you could be in with them one year and out the next.

Antonio Arias, the General Manager of Wisdom & Warter, saw the sales rise as John Charles became successful and immediately put up the price. Townend's would then cease to be competitive and would be delisted in some of the major customers. The sales fell and so the following year Antonio Arias came back and dropped the price; he thought Townend's could just walk back in with a lower price and get the trade back. Life, however, doesn't work like that. One of the most frustrating things for John Charles was that he had a first-class relationship with the wine buyer at Morrisons and he was selling thousands of cases per year when a Director of Gonzalez Byas, the holding company of Wisdom & Warter, went to Morrisons and persuaded them to have their own brand and offered them a very good price, undercutting Wisdom & Warter, which Morrisons naturally accepted.

At one blow Wisdom & Warter lost their biggest account in the UK.

LowCost was taken over by another group and Buyers' Own Brand replaced non-advertised brands such as Wisdom & Warter. Bodgas Lan was bought out and the new owner refused to pay a considerable sum of money due to the Company in respect of promotion and advertising allowances. John had been severely burned by the Keeling's case and was loathe to go to court with a foreign company but Townend's could not afford to write off the amount owing so they went to court and were eventually awarded £50k to include costs. National sales continued to decline; the only successful brand was Portal del Alto but by then John Charles was applying his talents and energy to building up the Wholesale Division.

Chapter 15:

A Political Incident

In May 1979, John was elected to Parliament for the Bridlington Constituency, with a large majority. This meant he was going to be an absentee landlord for the foreseeable future. He had anticipated his victory, as he was standing for a safe seat, and, therefore, in preparation for the day that he would enter Parliament, he decided in early 1979 that he would pass on the mantle of Managing Director to Gordon Clare, who was General Manager. Gordon was one of the Company's most loyal servants. He had started as an errand boy at the age of 14 at the Beverley Road shop, and later moved to work in the cellars at Cave Street. He joined the ATC at the beginning of the war and, when called up, automatically joined the RAF. He had a very good war; he trained as a wireless operator and he ended up as Warrant Officer, Senior Signals, on Sunderland flying boats.

When he returned in 1946 he went back into the cellars, where he was soon put in charge. His RAF career had made him lift his sights and he did not want to stay as a cellarman all his life. In 1954 he saw an advertisement in the *Hull Daily Mail* for a trainee stocktaker at Linsley & Co., a local firm of beer bottlers and wine and spirit merchants, which had recently been taken over by Joshua Tetley, the Leeds brewer, and he applied for the position. He got the job and left Townend's. He received a very good training and became a stocktaker. However, he missed the friendly atmosphere of a family firm and decided he did not want to spend his working life with a large impersonal public company. He went to see Charles and asked if he could return, not in the stores, but as a stocktaker. Townend's did not have a proper system at that time and had growing problems with branch stock shortages. Gordon offered to install a similar system to that which he had worked with at Linsley's. Charles agreed and Gordon came back and formed a Stocktaking Department with himself and one girl. He quickly solved the firm's stock problems and progressively expanded his responsibilities, until he became Branch Supervisor.

His big opportunity arose when Ken Wood left and he took over many of Ken's responsibilities and became Charles' 'Number 2' as Charles' son was still in the Air Force. When John came into the business, Gordon worked very well with the new young Director. After Charles' death he was responsible for the branches and the cellars and John eventually made him General Manager. His appointment as Managing Director was a well-deserved climax to a lifetime of loyal service to the Company and the family.

When John had only been in the House of Commons a relatively short time, an incident took place which had an impact on the Company. As John was a Chartered Accountant, he naturally took a great interest in financial matters and he asked the Whips if he could be part of the Standing Committee appointed to scrutinise the Finance Bill. The Whips acceded to his request on the basis 'one volunteer is worth two pressed men'. Being a new MP, and keen, John decided to get a copy of the Bill and read it before the Committee started. One night, when there was a Late Night Sitting, he sat in his office and started the formidable task. He had only got to page 5, when he saw:

'DEFINITION OF SCOTCH WHISKY' – There was to be a new definition of Scotch whisky, which was 'to be distilled and matured in Scotland for a minimum of three years'.

John immediately realised this would affect English whisky blenders, including his own company. The old definition was that 'Scotch whisky was whisky distilled in Scotland and matured for not less than three years'. English whisky blenders, therefore, filled casks of new whisky at the various distilleries, when it was manufactured, and brought them down immediately to their bonded warehouses, where they were stored for at least three years, when they were then blended and bottled. If the new legislation was passed, English whisky blenders would have to leave their new fillings in Scotland, at the distillery or at a Scottish Bond, and pay rental charges for three years. John decided that when the Committee reached this clause he would put the case of the English whisky blenders to the Committee. On rising to his feet he naturally declared his interest, as owning a Company that blended Scotch whisky in England. He made an impassioned speech, in which he told the Minister, Peter Rees MP, Chief Secretary of the Treasury, that his proposals were discriminatory, putting the English firms, which were much smaller family firms, and wine merchants, at a competitive disadvantage to the large, Scottish brand owners, mainly owned by big corporations. He finished off by asking the Minister 'how a new Conservative government, elected on a platform of helping and encouraging small businesses, could now be bringing in legislation aimed at disadvantaging small English wine merchants and independent brewers'.

The Minister was embarrassed, as he did not know of the existence of English blenders of Scotch whisky. He had not been adequately briefed by his Civil Servants and he wasn't pleased. He said he would investigate the points raised by the Honourable Member for Bridlington and, if what he said was correct, he would bring further proposals at the Report stage. Two days later, John was summoned to the Minister's office. The Minister was accompanied by a very embarrassed senior Civil Servant. He apologised to John for the fact that he had not been informed of the facts and told him he would like to hold a meeting with the Scottish Whisky Association, at whose request the new clause, changing the definition had been included, and a representative of the English blenders. He asked John if he could get the English blenders to appoint a spokesman. John agreed and said he would come back to the Minister's Secretary as soon as he had a name.

John now had to compose a list of English blenders. Before the war there had been dozens of small breweries and wine and spirit merchants who had blended their own whisky but he had no idea how many were left. He used all his contacts in the trade and, to his surprise and slight embarrassment, he found that, apart from his own company, there were only three others left. He spoke to them all and asked whom they would like to go to the meeting and be their spokesman. All three declined the

offer to attend themselves but asked John if he would represent them.

John informed the Minister's office and a meeting was arranged. The Minister opened the meeting by saying that, when he had originally approved the clause for insertion in the Bill, he did not know of the existence of the English whisky blenders. It had not been brought to his attention by either the Scotch Whisky Association or his Civil Servants. He said he had given an undertaking to the Honourable Member for Bridlington that he would take account of the interests of the English blenders, so he suggested that the representatives of the Scotch Whisky Association and John should withdraw into an adjoining room and see if they could do a deal. If they did not, he made it quite clear that the Clause would be taken out of the Finance Bill and the SWA would have to put forward their case the following year.

In the meeting, the SWA offered to pay the keeping costs in Scotland, for two years. John asked for three years; they agreed as they were desperate to get the clause in the Bill to stop foreigners buying new whisky and shipping it out of the UK before it was mature. As John was leaving, the senior Civil Servant said to John, 'You appreciate this matter has caused us some embarrassment; have you considered the balance of probability against this happening? There are over 50 million people in the UK. Out of that 50 million, four are English whisky blenders. There are 650 M.P.s and one of them is a whisky blender. Out of 650 M.P.s, 28 are on the Committee and that member happens to be on the Committee, and that Member actually read the Bill.'

This incident just shows how easy it is for legislation imposing burdens on industry and business to be passed without all the effects being taken into account. It also shows the importance of having M.P.s with experience and knowledge of industry.

The tragedy is, if this happened today, John would not be allowed to speak on the matter or lobby the Minister because new regulations forbid Members with an interest speaking on any matters affecting that interest. For example, beef farmers can no longer take part in agricultural debates on the question of cattle or beef marketing, or beef premiums. A grocer cannot speak on the food industry. Equally, a hotelier cannot speak on the tourist or hotel industry, even though their interests are declared in the Register of Members' Interests, and in any speech they make. When the new regulations came out, John went to see the Chief Official dealing with these matters. John said, 'I own a hotel. Is it a fact that I can no longer speak on matters affecting the hotel industry, or indeed, the tourist industry, generally?' 'Yes, that is correct,' said the official. 'Oh,' John replied 'what you are really saying is I should not be the Member for Bridlington.' 'How do you make that out?' said the official. 'Well,' John said, 'Bridlington is a tourist town with lots of hotels and B&B's. Its electors rightly think their MP should speak up for the town's businesses and industries. How can I represent them if I can't speak or ask a question? I am sure that one of the reasons they elected me was that my business experience would make me better able to represent their interests.' 'Oh,' said the official, 'I take your point; in your case I am sure we wouldn't take any action.' 'Can I have that in writing?' said John. 'That would not be possible,' replied the Civil Servant.

John, who strongly believes in maximum disclosure of interests and who fought against corruption when he was on the Hull Council, feels the new rules are ridiculous, because the personal experience of Members, whether in farming, fishing, business or the armed forces, is very important. Gagging Members with knowledge is playing to the hands of Ministers and Civil Servants, who don't like the idea of back bench M.P.s, experts in their own fields, picking holes in legislation, as John did in the episode of the English whisky blenders.

Chapter 16:

The 1980s

With the loss of the Keeling's case the Company was stagnant and profitability had collapsed. They had to review its strategy. John decided to return to its roots as a multiple retailer; in 1980 he cleared the decks and closed three unprofitable branches – Spring Bank, Anlaby and the Wine Centre in Carr Lane, the latter after a massive rent increase. He purchased John William Turner, the old-established wine shop in the market town of Driffield, where the Company had wanted to be represented for some time. In 1982 negotiations were started with North Country Brewery, formerly Hull Brewery, to buy its chain of 15 retail shops trading as Lambert Parker & Gaines but Townend's were outbid by Cellar 5. As a result of this disappointment John decided to expand by applying for new licences.

In that year Ron Mellor joined the Company as Head of the Retail Division; he had had experience with a big multiple chain of retail wine merchants and he was the first of three young men appointed in this decade whom John called 'his young Turks'. 1983, with the young head of retail settled in, was a year of great activity. Seven branches were opened, four in Lincolnshire – Broughton, Winterton, Barton and Brigg – one in Haxby near York, one in Market Weighton and one at Beverley – all new licences. This expansion was financed partly by the sale of Thomas Brothers, Elland. The expansion continued in 1984 when three new branches, Sutton, Gainsborough and Epworth, were opened and the adjoining unit to the Scunthorpe branch was rented and opened as The Home Brew and Greeting Card Centre. In that year another blow hit John. Ian Stamper, the Production Director, died and Gordon Clare, his Managing Director, retired.

The following year the Company tried yet another experiment and moved into franchising, firstly with the Haxby branch. By 1986 it was clear that the enlarged chain wasn't producing enough profit and a number of branches were marginal. The Company wanted to start

Phase 2 of the development of the Willerby Manor and required capital so it was felt that it should offer a parcel of 15 shops, including most of the poor ones, for sale. There were two serious bidders and the deal was finally done with Vaux Brewery, who owned the Blayney chain of shops, at a very good price. This was a coincidence, because Bob Blayney, John's friend from the Merchant Vintners, had sold his business to Vaux some years previously and had gone to live in Jersey. In October of that year a branch trading as The Wine Market was opened in purpose-built premises at the Willerby Manor. This was a large self-service store with ample car parking facilities. In 1987, the following year, Loncaster Wines in Hornsea was purchased.

The sale of 15 branches clearly affected Ron Mellor's view of John's desire to build up a large chain and in 1988 he resigned and rejoined a big company. He was replaced by a very enthusiastic hard-working Hong Kong Chinese, called Peter Wong. John was still keen to build up the retail chain again when any opportunity arose and in 1990 opened the Wine City in Hedon Road. It was a new concept, different from the House of Townend, and John had been very much influenced by his Finance Director, but it was never a great success.

The Wine Market at the Willerby Manor proved far too large for the turnover so it was moved into the cave-like premises of Raphael's restaurant, which had much more atmosphere than the old premises, which were turned into the Talbot Suite for the hotel and which could take up to 150 people. Peter Wong worked hard but the retail trade was getting more difficult and profits were harder to make, so he left to become the Manager of a large Morrisons supermarket.

In 1988 John was joined in the business by his son, John Charles, the fourth generation. John Charles always says he was indoctrinated into going into the business from an early age but did not acquire a love of wine until his gap year. He left Oundle a year before going to read Management Science at Warwick University. He wanted to go to Australia and 'bum around' for his gap year. That suggestion did not go down very well with his father, who left school at 17 and went straight into an accountant's office as an articled clerk, working all day

and studying all night. He asked his son, 'Who's going to pay for you?' 'I will work my way around Australia,' John Charles replied. 'And what about the cost of the flight?' asked his father. 'Surely, you would pay for that, Dad!' 'No,' said John. 'If you are going to have a gap year, do something that will benefit your career. Go to a non-English speaking country, go somewhere where you can learn a language.' John Charles reluctantly agreed, so his father made the arrangements through his contacts.

The first three months were spent in Bordeaux with Sichel's, where he worked in the cellar, and Peter Sichel arranged his digs, where nobody spoke English. The second three months were to be spent in Burgundy with Philip Marrion, Head of Chanson, Père & Fils in Beaune. Unfortunately, John Charles went skiing in the Christmas holidays and had an accident, severely damaging his knee, and by the time he was out of plaster he was only able to spend four or five weeks with Philip. He was very kind and sponsored John Charles on a course on wines of Burgundy run by the Comité Interproféssionel des Vins de Bourgogne (CIBB). He received the Diplôme d'Honneur. This was the start of his love affair with Burgundy. The next three months were probably the highlight of John Charles' year; he was a *stagiaire* at Moët & Chandon in Épernay. There were two other young men as *stagiares* and six *jeunes filles*. The ratio of boys to girls was very favourable, and, coupled with the fact that they all had a daily Champagne allowance, meant they had a ball. John Charles finished with a month in the Rhône and six weeks in Germany. He returned with a love of wine and was fluent in French. This was invaluable in his future career, for he was able to converse and negotiate with French growers in their own language – something his father could never do.

John Charles spent the next three years at Warwick University and finished with a very creditable 2:1 BSc in Management Science. During his University years he was training for the wine trade and during each summer vacation he would travel to a wine-producing district. One year he worked for George Duboeuf, the number-one firm in Beaujolais. Whilst he was there, one day he was driving to Romanèche-Thorins, when he momentarily forgot he was driving in France and had a crash with another car, but, fortunately, no one was hurt. Both cars were write-offs, but, when he got out of the wreck, he was horrified to find he had run into the Mayor of Fleurie.

When he left University he wanted to go and work for a wine firm in London to get experience. That would have been the best option. However, John had been away in Parliament for almost ten years; Gordon Clare, the former MD, had been retired for four years, the Keeling's case had had a debilitating effect and the Company was drifting. John said to his son, ' The business is beginning to suffer from having an absentee landlord for much of the week. If you join the Company in two or three years time I believe it could be a much smaller business.' John Charles accepted his father's view and joined the Company as soon as he left university. It was agreed that he should work in each department in turn so that he could have a good grounding in the trade. He started work at Red Duster House in the Order Department and after he had been there only a couple of weeks he said to his father, 'Did you know this is two businesses?' 'What do you mean?' asked John. 'It is a Monday and Friday business and a Tuesday to Thursday business. On Monday and Friday, when the staff know you are likely to be here, everyone comes on time and nobody stops work until 5.30 pm On Tuesday to Thursday people arrive late and the building is completely empty by 5.30 pm.'

After a month he came to see his father and said the man in charge of the Order Department should be got rid of. 'I agree with you,' said John. 'I am going on three weeks holiday on Saturday, you learn all you can and when I get back we will dismiss him (there was no employment legislation in those days) and you can take over.' 'We will take on a trainee, who you can train before you move on to the next department.' 'I don't agree,' said John Charles. 'Sack him now. Why waste three weeks' wages; I know I can do the job.' John was delighted at his son's confidence and willingness to take tough action. John Charles was a quick learner; he worked very closely with Peter Wong, the Head of the Retail Division, and, as has been mentioned in previous chapters, he played a major role promoting the national sales division and getting big accounts.

At the end of this decade John Charles heard at a meeting of Yorkshire wine merchants that 20 northern and Scottish universities negotiated a joint contract for the purchase of wines and that the current contract was held by a York firm. He was told the contract was worth £1 million. He found out who dealt with the contract and managed to get Townend's on the list of firms who would be asked to quote when the contract next came up for renewal. Townend's quoted and were put on the shortlist. Fortunately, the decision was not based purely on price; quality was to be considered. They were asked to submit samples for a blind tasting. Townend's came out on top and, although they had not submitted the cheapest quote, they were awarded the contract. This was a great coup and John was very impressed. It confirmed his view that he should step down from being Managing Director and hand over to John Charles, despite his tender age.

Chapter 17:

The Move into Wholesale

The Company had done a small, amount of wholesale when Jim Moggridge was Sales Director but John thought the Company had almost ignored the local wholesale business. So in 1982 he appointed John Charlton to be in charge of the small Cash & Carry but with a remit to develop local trade. He was responsible for an opportunity which arose with Tate Smith's, who were mineral manufacturers and beer wholesalers operating from Malton but who had no Wines and Spirits Department. After discussions a new Company, Tate, Smith and Townend was set up – 50% owned by Townend's and 50% by Tate Smith, to supply Tate Smith customers with wines and spirits. Tate Smith's got the orders and passed them on to Townend's, who assembled them. They were then taken in bulk to Tate Smith and delivered by their lorries.

In 1984 business had progressed to such an extent that Tate Smith and Townend's opened a Cash and Carry warehouse in Malton to service the business. The name was changed to Ryedale Vintners. Though not realised at the time, it later turned out this was the first step in the partnership being broken up. The Tate Smith's, having built the wine and spirit business on the back of Townend's stock, with no capital outlay, wanted to get the Townend's out. In 1989 Tim gave John an ultimatum – sell the shares or he would withdraw and let the business collapse. John was exposed; his Production Director had died, his Managing Director had retired and as he had nobody to run the business in Malton and his son, John Charles, had just joined the business and was being trained, he felt he had no alternative but to sell the shares.

This was another setback to John's plans for wholesale. In 1988 John Charlton resigned and was replaced by Graham Hollingsworth, a young man who was a sales representative with Yorkshire Fine Wines. His brief was to build up trade with hotels and restaurants, corporate business and the Cash & Carry. He did a reasonable job but one day in 1986, he dropped a bombshell on John's desk. He handed in his notice and informed John he was going to start his own business in opposition. This was yet another setback to John's hopes of establishing a growing, profitable wholesale trade.

John replaced him with Rod Prosser, who had been Manager of Lambert, Parker & Gaines, the wine and spirit division of Hull Brewery, who had joined the company a year earlier to fill the position of Warehouse and Bottling Manager. He had not settled into that job and jumped at the chance to be back at the sharp end of the wine business. As was inevitable, Graham Hollingsworth took quite a number of customers with him. However, at long last lady luck shined down on the Company for in 1990 Rod Prosser heard that Eddie Legard, a man who had been in the wine trade all his life, mainly with Bass, was looking for a job. Eddie was in his mid 50s and he was the main wine man for Bass in the East Midlands on the sales team; the rest were all beer salesmen. One day he was called to Head Office to see one of the directors. He had been very successful converting Bass beer accounts into buying wines and spirits and he thought he was going to be offered promotion. To his shock he was told a company decision had been made to downgrade wines and, therefore, he was faced with two choices: (1) becoming a beer rep, or (2) taking early redundancy. To one who had spent a lifetime devoted to wine, the thought of being a beer salesman was repugnant, so he took redundancy.

He was invited to attend an interview at Red Duster House with the two Townend's. The Company could not offer a large salary, so he was offered a modest salary with a good incentive with no limit. To Townend's surprise he accepted the offer with alacrity. He had the confidence to know that with his enormous number of customers and contacts he could sell sufficient wine to make the incentive very remunerative to him. He was an instant success and made a profit for the Company, almost from day one.

At last the Wholesale Division was on its way and, as John said, by sheer luck they had hit on a formula for recruiting the right people to make wholesale profitable. Instead of going for young men, who either pushed sales by cutting prices or moved on after a couple of years, there were a lot of older people being made redundant by large companies after takeovers who thought you were too old if over 50. Many of these men had enormous knowledge and experience and the contacts to bring in substantial amounts of business. John said he would take on any salesman, whatever the age, if they could bring in £¼m of business. Unfortunately, over the next three year Townend's could not find any more Eddie Legards and they continued with younger men, but not achieving quite the success they had hoped.

This failure was really disappointing for in the previous 15 years the rapid growth in the restaurant trade, with more and more people eating out, had seen a number of wine companies develop from small beginnings to become leading quality merchants. Other long-established companies had followed on the crest of this growing wave to build impressive businesses in this sector. In the north, the Yorkshire Fine Company was the number one company. However, the directors failed to reinvest their profits to finance the fantastic growth that they had achieved and eventually ran out of money. This, in due course, produced a number of opportunities for the House of Townend.

While the recession of the early 1990s caused problems in the wine trade, the fact that the House of Townend was not heavily involved in selling to hotels and restaurants proved to be fortuitous, as they were not saddled with a string of bad debts as many wine merchants were. At one stage in the early 1990s, Touche Ross, specialists in bankruptcies, administrations and liquidations, were the biggest UK hotel operators. House of Townend was, however, in a good position to make inroads into this sector, as the economy found its feet. John commented to John Charles that 'the big problem with the Company was that it wasn't very good at selling'. This had long been a bugbear of John's, as he knew that the House of Townend cellars contained wines that would rival any other merchant in the North. 'We are good at buying,' said John, 'we have as good a range as anywhere, but, apart from Eddie, we lack the right quality of salesmen.'

The big break was presented by the financial collapse of Yorkshire Fine Wines and its subsequent aborted takeover by the London-based wine merchant, Bibendum. Out of the blue, John Charles received a phone call from Alan Whitehead, the Sales Director, who had just returned from London after being made a casualty of the takeover. In his mid 40s, with a proven track record, he seemed to be the ideal person for the House of Townend Wholesale Division.

John Charles met Alan Whitehead the next day at the Willerby Manor. The meeting went well and Alan Whitehead agreed to join the Company. Soon afterwards John Charles was faced with a dilemma, as the other main wholesaler in the North, Pagendam Pratt, having got wind of Alan Whitehead's departure from Yorkshire Fine Wines, approached him with a better offer. Alan Whitehead approached John Charles and asked him to match the offer. John Charles said he would think about it and get back to him. A little miffed, John Charles consulted his father for his opinion on what to do. John was unequivocal. 'If you think he's the right man, match it. In the whole scheme of things it's not material, as he will only earn big money if he makes the sales (the package being heavily incentivised).' It was the quality of the list that had interested Alan; the wine range was impressive and the prices were such that he commented that 'selling in this company should be like falling off a log'.

Some time earlier, John decided that one way to speed up the growth of the Wholesale Division was to look around to see if there was any Yorkshire wine company that they could buy or merge with. He decided to approach Chennell & Armstrong, a York firm owned by the Butler-Adams family. He contacted the Managing Director, David Butler-Adams, whom he knew slightly, and discussions took place over lunch at the Willerby Manor. Progress was made and a second meeting was held with David and his brother, who was a chartered accountant. There was a lot of logic in the proposal and the House of Townend made an offer. Unfortunately, at about the same time Grierson Oldham & Adams, who had taken over the original Adams family business and had become the wine subsidiary of Trust House Forte, approached Chennell's. They wanted to take them over so they could become the distribution centre for their hotels in the North. The clincher was that they would take on all their staff and two large warehouses owned by Chennell's, which were of no interest to Townend. So, quite sensibly, the Butler-Adams family accepted this offer.

Yet again Townend's expansion plans for the Wholesale Division had been thwarted, but it was to be a blessing in disguise. They decided to continue looking and approached Cachet Wine, another private firm, based in Tadcaster. This company had been started by two partners, but they had recently split. The remaining partner, Graham Coverdale, entered into negotiations with Townend's. Agreement was reached and Townend's also offered Graham Coverdale and his corporate representative, Colin Freeman, positions in the sales team. Graham accepted and Townend's acquired an additional £¾m turnover. Earlier the same year, Colin Jones, a former colleague of Alan Whitehead's at Yorkshire Fine Wines, joined the Company to cover Derbyshire and the East Midlands.

The following year events again moved in the Company's favour; Granada made a bid for Trust House Forte and, during the bid battle, THF started selling its peripheral subsidiaries, including Grierson's, who were bought by Matthew Clark, a national composite wholesaler who had a very large trade in beer and minerals. John immediately thought David Butler-Adams would not want to spend the last few years of his career selling kegs of bitter; he was just not that sort of man and he felt he would retire. He remembered from his previous negotiations that Chennell's had had significant private trade, an area that Matthew Clark did not operate in, so it would be up for grabs. He telephoned David Butler-Adams and, over lunch at the Willerby Manor, David confirmed he would not be staying on with Matthew Clark. John asked him if he would consider working part-time to look after his private trade for Townend's. David declined the offer, saying he wasn't ready for semi-retirement and wanted to go on selling wine. That was music to John's ears and he quickly arranged a deal on the same principle as Eddie Legard's. By coincidence, at the same time Alan Whitehead heard that David Butler-Adams' top salesman, Mike Luke, did not like the new regime so he rang him up and persuaded him to join House of Townend on a similar package. Between the two of them they brought the major part of Chennell's old customers. Townend's got a large boost to turnover without having to pay a penny for goodwill. Both of them played a major part in the restructuring of the House of Townend from a major retailer to a major wholesaler. Mike Luke became the first member of the sales team to do £1 m turnover a year.

In two and a half years the sales team had gone from two to seven, all highly experienced, and Townend's were becoming a force to be reckoned with in Yorkshire and the East Midlands. The following year the sales force went up to eight when David Winterschladen, another ex-Yorkshire Fine Wine man, joined from Playford Ross. He was a member of The Vintners' Company, as was David Butler-Adams a future Master and, when John Charles subsequently became a Vintner, the House of Townend had three Vintners within the Company. As Master, David Butler-Adams was the first ever in 500 years to be elected from Yorkshire.

A year later talks took place between Phil Parrish, who operated a small one-man business in Driffield, East Yorkshire. His business was going nowhere so he joined the House of Townend. As with Cachet Wine there was no payment for goodwill; the Company took over stock and debtors. Phil joined the sales team with an additional responsibility for PR, but couldn't take the transition from being self-employed to being a member of a sales team and 18 months later he left.

Alan Whitehead had built up a small but useful business in the Lake District. John Charles thought the North West was a large and exciting, market, which he wanted to enter so in 1999 he appointed Andrew Wringe to cover Lancashire. At first Andrew did well but it seemed increasingly clear that the Company would not be able to become an important player in the region whilst all the orders were delivered from Hull and the level of service was below that offered to Yorkshire customers. The best solution to the problem was to buy a wholesaler with a warehouse and distribution into which House of Townend could feed its growing business. A firm in the North West was identified and John approached them. After long negotiations the owner decided he didn't want to sell for another four years, to avoid his paying over a share of any profit he made on disposal of the business to a former partner. Although no progress was made in the North West the Company now started negotiations with one of House of Townend's major competitors in Yorkshire. Unfortunately, the price the owner was asking was unrealistic, as he wanted Townend's to pay for any rationalisation benefits that they might make and, therefore, negotiations broke down. However, the Company had a coup when John Charles and Alan persuaded Alex Bussey, one of Pagendam Pratt's top salesmen, to join them.

Despite having no success in finding a firm to takeover in Lancashire, John Charles' ambitions to get a share of the lucrative market over in the North West was not diminished and he persuaded his father to agree to open a depot in the region, despite the additional costs, which would hit the bottom line for at least a couple of years. He started looking for premises and eventually found a modern warehouse of about 5,000/6,000 sq.ft, just off the motorway outside Warrington; it opened for business in September 2002. It was clear that the depot could not pay its way with just Andrew Wringe and Alan Whitehead's Lake District business, so it was decided to appoint another two salesmen.

Once more good fortune shone on the Company for Oddbins, a leading national retailer, who had a very good reputation for training staff, had been taken over by a French company, who, to their surprise, found they had acquired a significant wholesale business with 16 reps. As a retailer they were not up to speed with the wholesale trade, so they made all 16 redundant and invited them to apply for the four posts they were going to keep. Liam Bergin was recruited and shortly afterwards he recommended Rak Jain, one of the best of the 16 Oddbins' reps, who had been responsible for a turnover of over £2m. He joined House of Townend and after an early blip built up a strong business, particularly in Liverpool. Neil Goldie, the Oddbins' man in the Lake District, joined soon afterwards. He had been the Oddbins' shop manager in Kendal and knew the area

well. Neil was friendly with Andy Taylor, Oddbins' man in Newcastle, who was also unsettled due to the takeover. John Charles talked to him and he became the House of Townend's man in the North East.

The Company had recruited five salesmen from Oddbins and all but one settled down and played an important role in increasing the sales of the Wholesale Division. The opening of Warrington hit profits in the financial years 2002/3 and 2003/4 but break-even was achieved in the year 2004/5. By June 2005 an additional rep had been employed for the M6 corridor making four based at the Warrington depot.

Chapter 18:

Agency Mark II

By 1990 the National Sales/agency division had virtually withered on the vine and the only profitable agency remaining was Portal del Alto from Chile. The wholesale business had expanded by 1998 with a sales team of eight and it became clear that the House of Townend was the biggest customer of a number of small agency houses which shipped wines to the UK, selling on to UK merchants. Not only were House of Townend paying an agency mark-up, they also did not have control over their source of supply. A number of times, suppliers were unable to fulfil purchase orders due to poor stock holdings or, worse still, favouring an alternative customer.

John Charles and Alan Whitehead decided that the time was ripe to go back into the agency business with a different concept. Instead of looking for agencies from large producers, which would require volume sales to supermarkets groups, they decided they would represent small, medium-sized, independent growers who were as dedicated to quality as was the House of Townend and who would like to be represented by a family firm who could guarantee their wines would be introduced onto a lot of high-quality hotel and restaurant lists. This, the Townend's could do immediately by putting the wines through the existing wholesale network.

It was also decided to concentrate on New World and southern hemisphere wines because smaller wholesalers and wine merchants could buy economically from Europe but needed to go through an agency house if they could not ship whole containers from the rest of the world. Portal del Alto fitted perfectly into the profile. The benefit to the House of Townend would be immediate, for the agency wines sold to the House of Townend would be very profitable because there would be no selling costs. This would have an immediate impact on the bottom line. Philip Rhodes, a man of a mature age in the Eddie Legard mould, was recruited to sell to the independent trade. John Charles was looking for a trading name for his new venture. He didn't want to use House of Townend Agencies, so he decided to use the name Cachet Wine, which the Company had taken over but was not being used. In 1999 Alan went out to Australia to follow up a number of leads and managed to persuade Gary Crittenden of Dromana Wines to appoint Cachet Wine as his UK agents. The following year he had correspondence with Best's Wines, who were close great friends of Gary Crittenden's and he and John Charles went over and managed to take that agency away from another firm.

Philip Rhodes was very successful and paid his costs in the first year. In 2001 Barrie Howe, who had retired from Laurent-Perrier, joined Cachet to cover the North. In 2002 Philip Rhodes retired and was replaced by Tim Wildman, who was another ex-Oddbins man and quickly proved himself to be a great asset.

The formula was working and the search for further agencies was intensified. Australia became a fertile area and the following firms came to Cachet:

> Eagles Point, South East Australia
> Sandford Estate, Victoria
> Pauletts, Clare Valley
> Diamond Valley, Yarra Valley
> Ashton Hills, Adelaide Hills
> Main Ridge, Victoria
> Hugo Winery, McLaren Vale
> Clarendon Hills
> Killara Park Estate, Yarra Valley
> Craneford Wines, South Australia
> Hamilton's Ewell, Barossa Valley
> Zema Estate, Coonawarra

New Zealand proved more difficult but in 2003, following a visit by the Chairman, Cachet Wine was appointed agents for Hawkes Bay Estate, owned by C J Pask.

Alan had had correspondence with Rockburn Wines, which had been founded by Dick Brunton, a huge surgeon from Invercargill; he had been backed by three Auckland business men John met him in Queenstown, which was the nearest town to his vineyards. He was well over six-feet tall and had played provincial rugby, almost making the All Blacks. He and one of his investors from Auckland had dinner with John and Jennifer; it was a very good night and a mutual interest in rugby helped the conversation flow. Whilst they were having coffee the partner from Auckland said, 'Dick, these are the sort of people we need to have as our UK agents.' Townend's were delighted to be appointed agents, as Rockburn in Otago produced world class Pinot Noir. The following year, Waipara Hills, Marlborough, joined the Cachet Wine stable after its agents went experienced financial problems.

In South Africa, after a false start John Charles found the Avondale Estate in Paarl owned by the Grieve family, owners of the hugely successful Vital Health Foods Empire in Cape Town. John Grieve set about restoring the Avondale Wine farm in Paarl. With the Parrl Mountains providing a stunning backdrop, the Grieve's have built an ultra-modern winery that any winemaker in the world would be impressed with.

There has been a slight drift back to Europe. The old established family Port firm of Poças appointed Cachet Wine as agents in 1999 and the Company became the main importers of 'La Citadelle' Luberon, owned by the Mayor of Ménerbes, whose winery John can see from the terrace of his house in Provence. Cachet Wine also distributes the great Rhone wines produced by Daniel Brunier, the proprietor of Vieux Télégraphe.

In 2004 the Company launched a new range of varietals, sourced from various producers in France and Italy. The aim was to offer the finest example of each varietal, expressing the characteristics that are typically associated with each grape. Central to the launch was the style of packaging and the brand name. The wines were marketed under the name 'Pure'. So often with brands, the packaging suggests great things but ultimately leaves the consumer disappointed; the aim of 'Pure' is to give the full package. This is a return to the Company's roots because for most of its history it has believed in having its own brands, from the 1930s with Port, Sherry, rum and whisky, and later many wines were branded with either the Company's brand or the Merchant Vintners'.

An example of the work put in to ensure the quality of the product was in the sourcing of the Sauvignon Blanc. John Charles has always been a great admirer of the wines produced by the Plaimont Co-operative in south west France. During one of his visits he asked to taste the samples from the tanks of Sauvignon, which was used in the blend of the Côtes de Gascognes wines, produced by the Plaimont Co-operative. Following the tasting, in which the wines showed fantastically well, John Charles asked about the possibility of taking this Sauvignon and bottling it as an individual cépage. 'No chance!' was the reply. The haggling, cajoling and persuading went on without success for a couple of hours. Finally, when Monsieur Dubosc, the founder of the Plaimont Co-Operative, arrived, much to the dismay of his managers, Monsieur Dubosc agreed, given the long-standing association that Plaimont had had with the House of Townend. It is very rare that one particular wine can either open or save accounts, but time and time again the 'Pure' Sauvignon has done just that. Plaimont also supply a Chardonnay and their Rosé, under the name 'Pure Pink', while the Shiraz and Merlot are supplied by Alain Grignon at LGI and the Pinot Grigio supplied by the Girelli family in Trentino, north-east Italy. At the time of writing, the Company is in the process of moving the whole range into stelvin, which will see a further boost to sales.

Chapter 19:

1991 to the Centenary

The last 15 years have not been easy for the Company, especially for the Managing Directors of our two Companies, for it has been a period of great change.

At the start of the period the core business was still the chain of 14 retail branches. The old national sales division was still operating, having been given the kiss of life by John Charles, and the growing wholesale division was still relatively small. Central to the success of the redefined business was the quality and the range of the list – always a gripe with the Warehouse and Accounts Departments; the number of lines grew. The individuality and quality of wine being continually introduced had a positive effect from the sales angle. The reason for buying from House of Townend was for quality; whilst the pricing was fair, the issue of price was never part of the sales pitch. Good restaurants bought the best quality steaks – surely they should be matched with a wine of equal quality.

The business trips that John enjoyed over the years had changed beyond all recognition. John recalls the days when he visited Burgundy with other Merchant Vintner members, such as Richard Tanner and Derek Balls. 'We would visit one supplier in the morning, have an in-depth tasting, followed by a jolly good lunch. We would then squeeze in a visit in the afternoon, followed by a jolly good dinner!' By the mid-1990s, things had changed. John asked if he could join John Charles for a day in Burgundy, on his way back from Strasbourg as part of his role on the Council of Europe. On a cold, rainy November day, John stumbled from one cold cellar to another, visiting seven domaines in the day, with only a quick sandwich for lunch. By six o'clock he was dead on his feet and his palate had been on strike for several hours! His role was still pivotal, however. John Charles had been badgering Anthony Sarjeant, a Burgundian broker, for an allocation from the great Puligny Domaine of Vincent Leflaive. Before getting in the car that morning, John Charles said to his father, 'Your job today

is to wear Anthony Sarjeant down and get him to agree to give House of Townend an allocation.' As soon as the door closed, he started the softening-up process. After each and every call the slamming of the car doors was followed by, 'Now, what about Leflaive?' By lunchtime, Anthony Sarjeant had given every excuse in his armoury; the badgering showed no effect and by mid-afternoon an embarrassing air engulfed the car. It was tangible to all occupants, apart from the one in the front passenger seat. On and on he went, 'When? Why not? Only a few cases. We buy from some of the top domaines in Burgundy. Surely Leflaive would want to be amongst them on our list.' By five o'clock the result was in the bag. John had hardly opened his mouth after another car door shut when Anthony Sarjeant shouted back, 'Oh, for Christ's sake, you can have your bloody Leflaive!' 'Good,' said John. 'I'll shut up now.'

In 1991 the Company parted company with their Finance Director. He was replaced by Pat Mole, a lady chartered accountant. With Peter Wong, a Hong Kong Chinese, already the Retail Director, the Chairman was able to say they could not be accused of being prejudiced because the only non-family directors were a woman and a member of an ethnic minority. Unfortunately, that did not last very long. Pat found that being a busy finance director and having a young daughter did not go together so she left to work at the local university where she could have more family-friendly hours and much longer holidays.

She was replaced by Peter Rainger, who stayed with the Company until 2004. Peter had been Company Secretary/Accountant but it was decided this was a key post and, therefore, should be changed to Company Secretary/Finance Director designate. Angus Whitehead, no relation to Alan, was appointed and within a matter of months made a significant impact on the financial reporting and was appointed Group Finance Director in 2005.

When the opportunity arose the Company still expanded the retail chains, and branches were opened in Hull at Chanterlands Avenue in 1993 and Holderness Road in 1998. Generally, however, the pressure on the viability of independent wine shops continued to be affected by growing competition from supermarkets, which opened longer hours and had a massive improvement in their range and the quality of their offering. Licences became available almost on demand, even petrol stations started getting them and the Company faced the increasing problems and cost caused by the breakdown of law and order. The Company tried to stop the decline in the profitability of the Retail Division by rebranding the chain in 1997 as Booze Brothers, in place of House of Townend. Unfortunately this did not affect the long-term decline in profitability and a decision was taken to progressively withdraw from the retail shop business and restructure the Company to focus on wholesaling.

It was decided that this would have to be done in stages as the wholesale business had to expand to be able to take over more and more of the overheads. Obviously unprofitable branches were closed or disposed of first; Cottingham and Brigg were sold to Rhythm 'n' Booze in 1997, Withernsea was closed in 1999, Epworth in 2000, and the freehold properties sold. Wine City followed in 2001, Ferriby in 2003, the Wine Market at the Willerby Manor in 2004, Chanterlands Avenue and Beverley Road in 2005. Closing Beverley Road was a very difficult decision as it was where the Company started and it would have been nice to keep it open until after the centenary. However, it was losing money and taking a lot of management time. One reason the Company has survived for so long is that when circumstances were difficult the Directors never funked making difficult but necessary decisions. It is expected that by the start of the centenary year the number of branches will be reduced to two or three, all profitable.

The growth of convenience stores started to take off in the United Kingdom. The Sutton branch, which sold groceries, had developed into a successful convenience store, so the Company decided it would extend this new format. In 2001 Holderness Road was enlarged and refitted as a convenience store and Barton was given the same treatment in 2002. This was another retail initiative that didn't work out and Barton reverted to a pure wine shop.

The Company has not, however, completely turned its back on the general public. It was decided to start and progressively replace some of the retail branch contributions by going into Mail Order. This was a logical decision as the Company had large stocks of fine wines and produced one of the best Lists in the north of England. John Charles' wife, Susie, joined the Company to launch this new project and brought with her a certain experience in PR and marketing.

Trade slowly build up and gradually the department was recognised by wine writers. In 1997 John Charles, whilst visiting his father's house in Provence, found a very good Cabernet Sauvignon made by La Citadelle winery in the Lubéron. This was written up in the *Guardian* by the wine correspondent, Michael Gluck, who made it his 'Superplonk'. This had a big impact and resulted in sales of hundreds of cases of this wine over just a couple of weeks. Naturally, the Company was delighted and thought it had made a real break-through but to their horror, six weeks later, Gluck wrote an article in the *Guardian* saying it had been drawn to his attention that the Chairman of the firm whose wine he had recommended was John Townend, the 'racist' MP, and that he urged all his readers to boycott the House of Townend until John was forced to resign and sell his shares. He said he was also going to write to all the wineries supplying the House of Townend, urging them to refuse to supply the Company. Townend's also learnt that he had written to all the wine writers urging them not to give the Company any publicity whatsoever.

Thankfully, not a single supplier took any notice of this vicious campaign, but there is no doubt that the boycott of the wine writers, which resulted in a virtual blackout of PR, severely affected the growth of the Mail Order department for a number of years. John was advised that Gluck's comments were libellous, so he went to a top libel lawyer in London, who advised him that he had definitely been libelled and that he had a good case, but if he sued it would take three years out of his life. No one could guarantee winning, and, as Conservative M.P.s were not the most popular with juries at the time, if he happened to lose, the costs would be in excess of six figures. He said the alternative was to use the Press Complaints Council to try and get an apology.

After his experience with the Keeling's case the last thing John wanted at the age of 65 years was living on a knife-edge for three years. He took the lawyer's advice and issued a complaint to the Press Council. He did not get an apology but it was to be expected that the Politically Correct Great and the Good would not find in favour of an outspoken MP.

This was not the only occasion when the Company was victimised for John's outspoken views. About the same time the Hull Probation Service cancelled a conference they had booked at the Willerby Manor because John was Chairman of the Company. A few years previously Townend's had won a two-year contract to supply Hull Corporation with its wines and spirits for its outlets, which included the New Theatre, the Guildhall and the City Hall. This was cancelled after one year because the Labour Council objected to John's politics. John wanted to sue them for breach of contract but John Charles did not want the hassle and the publicity.

The final, vicious attacks of the Politically Correct affected John personally, rather than the Company. He had been invited to be the next National President of the Wine and Sprits Association of Great Britain, the industry's main trade association, on whose Council he had served for a number of years. However, following the attacks in the press concerning his opposition to multi-culturalism and his belief that all illegal asylum seekers should be expelled quickly from the UK, this invitation was withdrawn. Throughout this difficult time both John Charles and Alexandra loyally stood shoulder to shoulder with their father on these issues as they considered the attack on their father was an attack on an Englishman's traditional right of free speech. John Charles insisted that the Company resign from membership of the Wine and Spirit Association in protest at the way his father had been treated.

John is surprised, but naturally pleased, that so many of his views that were condemned in 1997 are becoming more and more accepted. Even Trevor Phillips, the Chairman of the Commission for Racial Equality, says multi-culturism has been bad for the UK and believes that what we now need is integration – almost exactly John's words – and the overriding majority of the country believe illegal or failed asylum seekers should be sent back in weeks.

John had always had a policy of buying any adjoining property that came up for sale, providing the price was right. In 2001 a large warehouse of 16,260 square feet, next door to Red Duster House came on the market. It was a big 'box', ideal for storage and use of forklift trucks. John suggested they should buy it but John Charles was very keen to acquire a depot in Lancashire at that time and was not very interested in investing more money in Hull, which was not good geographically for distribution. He did toy for sometime with the idea of moving from Hull altogether and getting premises near the M62 in the West Riding. He was influenced by the fact the 95% of the business is now outside Hull. This is surprising, as the House of Townend is the only surviving wine merchant of any size in Hull. 'No man is a prophet in his own town'.

However, by the Christmas of that year, due to the growing wholesale business and the fact that the Company was supplying a significant number of containers of beer to a grocery chain through a third party, the Company was finding it just did not have enough space to handle the increasing number of containers coming in and going out. As the adjoining property was still unsold after nine months on the market, Townend's decided to make an offer well below the asking price. When their agent approached the vendor they were surprised when he said it had been sold only the previous week. Fortunately, in conversation he found out what the other party had bid.

When he told John and John Charles, they were shocked because they both now realised the implications of letting it slip through their fingers. They decided to tell the agent to put in a higher offer than that of the purchaser and, to their delight and relief, the other party refused to increase its offer, because they felt they had been gazumped and so Townend's bought it. The purchase meant they had a much more efficient method for handling goods and preparing orders. The space occupied had doubled so that the Company now had the physical capacity to double its turnover. It also meant the Company was now committed to Hull for the foreseeable future, despite its unsatisfactory, geographical position. The cost of replacing the existing freehold property, which had been bought at good prices near the motorways in the centre of the country, would run into several million pounds.

When the Duty Paid and Order Picking department moved into the new building, the space available was adapted to make an enlarged Cash & Carry department with a much bigger car park. The sales have increased and it now makes a useful contribution.

It is to be expected that everything has not always been plain sailing when a firm has been in existence for 100 years. All businesses have their ups and downs. There are economic cycles, recessions and competition to be faced.

On two occasions Townend's faced the possibility that the Company would not survive. The first was in the 1920s when the founder foolishly signed a guarantee for a fishing company, without fully understanding the meaning of the phrase 'joint and several'. The second was when Allied Brewers won the Advocaat case.

The firm survived and, as the present Chairman enjoys reminding people, 'that's more than can be said for Allied Breweries, who no longer exist, having been taken over last year and cannibalised'. The firm also survived the adverse effects of the Chairman's political life and the boycott by the wine writers. Today, the current company, with its two trading subsidiaries, is stronger financially than in any time in its history.

Over the century the firm has been involved in practically every activity involved within the liquor industry. It started as a spin-off from the founder's beer-bottling business and from the very beginning was both a retail and a wholesale wine and spirit merchant, quickly becoming a bottler. It later became an importer, blender of rum and whisky, a compounder of gin and vodka, manufacturer of 'Keeling's Old English Advocaat' and cocktails such as 'Green Goddess', an operator of pubs, a wine bar, an outside caterer, a Cash & Carry operator and a Mail Order merchant; in fact, as the Chairman said: 'If he thought he could turn a profit in any activity connected with the trade, he would have a go, especially

if it resulted in a better margin for the existing business.' The only activity he never got involved with was producing wines from the Company's own vineyards. That remains a challenge for future generations in the next hundred years.

Circumstances have changed, and regulations have made life more difficult for the small operator in so many fields. It became imperative to rationalise and specialise. Bottling, blending and manufacturing went 15 years ago. The last pub and the wine bar in Elland were sold to pay for the cost of the Advocaat cases and most outside catering went as Alexandra concentrated on the hotel. The slimmed-down firm now consists of the wine company, which is involved in wholesaling and importing, a couple of retail shops, a Mail Order department, Cash & Carry, a Bonded warehouse and the hotel company which operates the Willerby Manor.

As the centenary approaches, the Company, under the day-to-day management of the fourth generation, is progressing well. John Charles has successfully changed the core business of the wine company, which was the chain of retail wine shops, and replaced it with wholesale business dealing with the top to middle end of the market, from the Scottish Borders down to Stratford on the east side and Birmingham on the west side, with a sales team of 13. With distribution depots in Hull and Warrington, customers are now served by the Company's own fleet of vans. The rapid expansion of the wholesale business has been due to three factors:

1. The high quality of the sales team, most of whom are very experienced and knowledgeable about the wine trade.

2. The quality and range of the wines, the vast majority of which are selected personally by the directors travelling abroad, and imported direct from the wine makers into the Company's own Bonded warehouse at Red Duster House, York Street.

3. High quality service that is given to the customer. With £2 million worth of stock held in the Company's Bond and warehouses, the incidence of items 'out of stock' is much lower

than that of competitors. Enthusiastic and dedicated staff, from the salesmen to the Telesales girls and the warehousemen and drivers, aim to make the life of the hotelier and restaurateur a little easier. More and more the Company is seen as the leading quality wine and spirits wholesaler in the North of England.

Cachet Wine, the Agency company, with two dedicated salesmen, covers the whole country and is growing steadily as the firm represents more and more small and medium-sized top quality producers. The Mail Order and Private trade department has got over its problems and is now growing well. The Cash & Carry is becoming increasingly popular with the licensed trade as the Company is no longer seen as a competing retailer. The Corporate side is also increasing due to the wide variety and the quality of the products and good prices.

The Willerby Manor Hotel, run by Alexandra, has been described by John as 'The Jewel in the Crown' and Alex as the 'Company Cash Cow'. According to the AA ratings, it is the best hotel in the area and has two rosettes for its excellent food. It has without doubt the best banqueting operation in the area and its Health Club is of a very high quality. Over the years investment has been poured into the hotel in order to achieve its present pre-eminence in the county and, as the centenary year starts, an additional 12 bedrooms will be about to come on stream.

The success of any business depends first of all on its people. Townend's has always tried to recruit good people and keep them. They are very proud of the Number 10 Club, which is made up of all the members of the firm who have served ten years or more. In 2006 the membership will amount to 46. Of these, 13 are from the Willerby Manor. This is something the hotel is very proud of, because the industry is noted for a high turnover of staff.

Many people have played a major part in the growth and success of the business and there is only space to mention a few. The first that comes to my mind is the great character, Charlie White ('Whitey'), the Company's first employee. Another is Ken Wood, the second employee, who started in the 1930s as a warehouse boy and ended up in the 1950s as General Manager. Gordon Clare joined in 1938 as an errand boy and retired as Managing Director. Walter Redhead, 'van man extraordinaire', ran outside bars. John Mercer, who served 42 years, was the best van driver in the trade; both he and Walter worked long after their retiring age, part-time. John Boardley, had 45 years service as Stocktaker and in charge of the Bond while Steve Wood, was Office Manager, with 32 years service. Jonathan Preston served in many departments, and is now the Purchasing Manager. In recent years Alan Whitehead has played a significant part in building up the Wholesale Division, as have Mike Luke and David Butler-Adams, two of the finest wine sales executives in the country. Many, many more have given years of loyal service, including Louise Taylor and Darryl Stewart and Branch Managers Walter Sigsworth and the late Harry Beacock. At the Willerby Manor, Derek Baugh was the inspiration and David Roberts has given invaluable support to Alex for may years.

No family business can survive unless in every generation there are members of the family both capable and willing to carry on the torch. The House of Townend is fortunate that two members of the fourth generation have successfully carried on the work of former generations. After 100 years and four generations, John, still the Chairman, dreams of at least one of his ten grandchildren being the fifth generation. But who knows if his determination to keep the House of Townend going will be inherited by the fifth generation?